×Leckie
the education publisher
for Scotland

SNAP
REVISION
ENGLISH
LANGUAGE

Build your BGE S1-S3 English Skills

REVISE TRICKY TOPICS IN A SNAP

David Cockburn

Published by Leckie
An imprint of HarperCollins*Publishers*
1 London Bridge Street
London SE1 9GF

HarperCollins*Publishers*
1st Floor, Watermarque Building, Ringsend
Road, Dublin 4, Ireland

ISBN 9780008528089

First published 2022

10 9 8 7 6 5 4 3 2 1

British Library Cataloguing in Publication Data.

A CIP record of this book is available from the British Library.

Commissioning Editors: Gillian Bowman and Clare Souza
Author: David Cockburn
Project Editor: Peter Dennis
Typesetting: QBS Learning
Cover designers: Kneath Associates and Sarah Duxbury
Printed and bound in the UK using 100% Renewable Electricity at CPI Group (UK) Ltd

Author acknowledgements:
I owe an inestimable debt to Margaret Insch, sadly no longer with us, who was instrumental in clarifying my thoughts about grammar and how to teach it effectively; I should also like to thank Alison Campbell for her extensive knowledge about language, written and spoken, and her unswerving encouragement; and, most importantly, I should like to thank Kevin Cockburn, without whole endless support and patience this book would never have been written. I should also very much like to thank the team at Leckie for their professionalism and care which is always such a joy to experience.

ACKNOWLEDGEMENTS

p. 8, Jonathan Raban, 'For Love and Money', Eland Publishing; p. 12, Laurie Lee 'As I Walked Out One Midsummer Morning', Penguin Books; p. 39, Carol Ann Duffy, 'Stealing', Picador, 2016; p. 49, John Steinbeck, 'Of Mice and Men', Penguin Books; p. 52, 74, Gerrit L Verschuur, 'Impact! The Threat of Comets and Asteroids', Oxford University Press; p. 53, John Cooper and Hannah Greig, 'Why did the 1605 gunpowder plot fail? 9 big questions about the conspiracy to blow up parliament', BBC History Extra! Nov. 2017; p. 57, Steve Connor, 'Can an ape learn to be human?', The Independent, Aug. 2011; p. 58, Laurie Lee, 'Cider with Rosie', Penguin Books; p. 60, Ernest Hemingway, 'The Sun Also Rises', Penguin Books; p. 66, Mark Smith, 'How Nostalgia Could Save the Future', The Herald, Jan. 2022; p. 68, Matthew Syed. Adapted from 'Missing penalty not end of world but a chance to learn more about life', The Times, 9 July 2014. News Syndication. The Times, July 2014; p. 78, Christina Patterson, 'We'd all benefit from encouraging children to go outside and take risks' The Guardian, p. 78, 79, Ross Martin, 'Square Roots', The Herald, Feb. 2013; Rebecca McQuillan, 'Hey guys, do you think we could all stop talking American?', The Herald, Dec. 2021.

The author and publisher are grateful to the copyright holders for permission to use quoted materials and images.

Every effort has been made to trace copyright holders and obtain their permission for the use of copyright material. The author and publisher will gladly receive information enabling them to rectify any error or omission in subsequent editions. All facts are correct at time of going to press.

MIX
Paper | Supporting responsible forestry
FSC
www.fsc.org   FSC™ C007454

Contents

ebook

To access the ebook version, visit collins.co.uk/ebooks and follow the step-by-step instructions.

Introduction

The two main purposes of this book are to teach you:

(a) to analyse the ways in which writers use sentence structure to create effects;

(b) to write in sentences that are grammatically accurate.

To achieve these two purposes, we need to begin with all aspects of grammar. We will start with the basics – word classes such as nouns, prepositions, adverbs, word order – and we will show the ways in which sentences are structured. We will also deal with what is meant by tone and register.

You might ask – why bother about grammar? Well, there is one main reason why grammar matters:

- since the main purpose of language is to express clearly and precisely our thoughts and feelings and to communicate effectively with others, the more accurately we can do that the more successfully we will be able to read, speak, and write.

Grammar is the system of rules that governs the way language is put together. There are two terms you need to be aware of:

- grammar – the set of rules by which the *whole language* is put together; and
- syntax – the way in which an *individual sentence* has been put together.

The English language is made up of words – nouns, verbs, adjectives, adverbs, and so on. We will begin by looking at the various types of words used – that is, we'll look at the techniques used to classify words.

There are many other types of word classes, all of which you will learn about. We will cover them all: adjectives, adverbs, prepositions, pronouns, and, of course, verbs. Most of these word classes you use every day, but in this book you will learn how to use them exactly and accurately.

Answers

Answers to the Quick tests and a glossary of useful terms are available online. Visit

https://collins.co.uk/pages/scottish-curriculum-free-resources-leckie-snap-revision

Nouns

We'll start with nouns. You already know that nouns are the names of things, and you probably also know that nouns can be the names of emotions, feelings and ideas. Nouns can be the names of people or pets or towns or countries. There are also collective nouns. We'll look at each of these four types of nouns in the table below.

Nouns	Function	Example
Concrete or common nouns	The name of something that actually exists, that you can see or hear or smell or taste or touch.	lion, human, football, pitch, star, chair, moon, chocolate, roar, perfume, church, scarf, bag, trainers, nail, stapler, mist, smoke, noise, rock, paper, music, clouds
Abstract noun	The name of an emotion or feeling – something that you cannot recognise with your senses. Such nouns often end in -ness or -dom or -ment.	happiness, sadness, tiredness, grief, excitement, hearing, eyesight, loveliness, loneliness, beauty, nosiness, cleanliness, uprightness, merriment, backwardness, epilepsy, intelligence, boredom, freedom, martyrdom, kingdom, government, conflict, rebellion, bureaucracy, existence, spring, summer, autumn, winter
Proper noun	A person's name, the name of a town or city or region or country. All proper nouns must begin with a capital letter.	Aberdeen, Dundee, Fife, Scotland, Fiona, Europe, Hamlet, Emmerdale, The Herald, Treasure Island
Collective noun	The name given to any group – animals, objects; a collection of things taken as a whole.	A *pride* of lions, a *pack* of wolves, a *herd* of cows, a *flock* of sheep, a *parliament* of owls, a *skein* of geese (when flying), a *gaggle* of geese (when on the ground), a *troop* of monkeys, a *bunch* of flowers

Countable and uncountable nouns

The easiest way to define countable nouns is that they have both singular and plural forms (for example egg/eggs, pizza/pizzas, dog/dogs) whereas uncountable nouns have only a singular form (milk, fish, helium, petrol, dust).

You need to know about countable and uncountable nouns for three reasons:

1. When to use *fewer* or *less*.

   Use the word *fewer* with countable nouns (plurals) and *less* with uncountable nouns – e.g. 'There were fewer apples in the bowl than expected.'

   Use the word *less with* uncountable nouns – e.g. 'There was less money in my account than I thought.'

2. When to use *number of* and *amount of / a lot of*.

   Use *a number of* with countable nouns (plurals) – e.g. 'I have visited that place a number of times.'

   Use *amount of* and *a lot of* with uncountable nouns – e.g. 'I was shocked by the amount of homework I was given.'

   'It took a huge amount of time to finish the race.'

   'There was a lot of dust on the table.'

3. When to use *much* and *more*.

   Use *more* with plurals – e.g. 'There are more penguins in the zoo these days.'

   Use *much* with uncountable nouns – e.g. 'There was much laughter in the room.'

   'I don't have much milk.'

Quick Test 1

Decide which is the right word to use in the following sentences:

(i)   I haven't got much/many pencils.

(ii) They went to the cinema a number of/an amount of times.

(iii) There were fewer/less pupils sitting in the library.

(iv) We saw that there were fewer/less sparrows this year.

(v)   We haven't much/many chocolates left.

Compound nouns

Compound nouns are formed by two nouns, which are used so frequently together that they form a compound noun. Compound nouns can be made up of (1) two separate words; (2) two words that are hyphenated; (3) or two words that have been together so long that they form a single word.

'Cat' is a noun as is 'flap', and together they form the compound noun 'cat flap'. Other examples are:

- dog bowl
- window cleaner
- arts centre
- pedestrian crossing
- egg rolls

Compound nouns can also be formed by an adjective and a noun. For example, 'full moon' is made up of the noun 'moon' modified by the adjective 'full' but used so frequently together that the term 'full moon' is regarded as a compound noun. Other examples are:

- past life
- washing machine
- changing rooms
- young man
- old age

Often, the two words begin life hyphenated, then end up as one word: for example, 'door-mat' eventually became 'doormat'. Other examples are:

With hyphens:

- check-up
- daughter-in-law
- dry-cleaning
- well-being
- six-pack

Without hyphens:

- checkout
- chalkboard
- smartphone
- toothpaste
- midsummer
- dishwasher

1. (i) Give 10 examples of common nouns.
   (ii) Give 10 examples of proper nouns.
   (iii) Give 10 examples of collective nouns (you might have to research this one).
   (iv) Give 10 examples of abstract nouns.

2. Using the following nouns, write down any compound nouns that come to mind:
   - drive, film, garage, pencil, pen, paper, earth, sea, television, telephone, electric, problem, history, traffic, school, water, clock, town, generation.

3. Identify and classify the nouns in the following sentences. The first one is done for you:
   a. Andrew was able to see a tiger when on safari.
      Andrew   –   proper noun
      tiger   →   common noun
      safari   –   common noun
   b. You will hear the squeals of delight from the children as we climb on board a vintage steam train.
   c. Alison always claims that honesty is the best policy.
   d. You can hear the hooves of the reindeer as they clatter over the roofs of all the houses.

4. Identify and classify all the nouns in the following extract from an essay by Jonathan Raban:

It's wrong to say, as people always do, that London does not use its river. The Thames has never been the city's chief point of focus like the Seine in Paris or the Grand Canal in Venice. Yet London, no less than Venice or Paris uses its river to define itself. The Thames marks the edge of things. It is what makes north London north and south London south. Like a twisty ruler, it measures out the intricate social and economic gradations between the east and west of the city. But the Thames is a boundary, not a thoroughfare, and like all boundaries it is there for people to turn back from.

Plural nouns

This is where it gets interesting! In English we form the plural in a variety of ways, the simplest of which is to add an -s to the stock word:

Singular	Plural
horse	horses
dog	dogs
house	houses
desk	desks

With nouns ending in x, s, x, z, ch, English forms the plural by adding -es:

Singular	Plural
tax	taxes
buzz	buzzes
church	churches
bus	buses
fox	foxes

With words ending in y, to form the plural change the y to i and adding -es:

Singular	Plural
spy	spies
academy	academies
absurdity	absurdities
agency	agencies
commodity	commodities
opportunity	opportunities

Words which end in -*o*, add *es* to form the plural:

Singular	Plural
echo	echoes
hero	heroes
tomato	tomatoes

If the noun ends in -*io* or -*yo* just add *s*:

Singular	Plural
patio	patios
studio	studios
embryo	embryos

There is a really old way to form the plural and we still use it: add -*en* to the noun:

Singular	Plural
ox	oxen
child	children

Strangely some nouns have only a plural form:

trousers	doldrums	goggles
shorts	clothes	binoculars
riches	amends	glasses
scissors	news	spectacles
electronics	leggings	pyjamas
belongings	outskirts	surroundings

Watch out for the word 'news': although it has only a plural form it takes a singular verb: for example:

The BBC News *is* broadcast every evening at six o'clock.

And even more oddly, some nouns have only a singular form:

aircraft	deer
sheep	fish

If the noun in the singular form ends in -f, we often (but not always) change the f to a v and add -es:

Singular	Plural
hoof	hooves
loaf	loaves
life	lives
wife	wives
half	halves

BUT watch out for:

Singular	Plural
roof	roofs
chief	chiefs
spoof	spoofs

Another method of forming the plural is to change the vowel:

Singular	Plural
woman	women
man	men
tooth	teeth
analysis	analyses
foot	feet
crisis	crises
mouse	mice

1. Form the plural of the following words:

   actress, knife, lady, library, cactus, taxi, hoof, pants, roof, mother-in-law, step-son, firefighter, police-constable, sheep, echo, penny, tomato, tooth.

2. Check for yourself the plural of:

   alga, larva, caesura, crisis, neurosis, chateau, bureau, cactus, formula, millennium, stadium, medium, fresco, addendum, criterion, jeans, phenomenon.

3. Write down at least FOUR ways of forming a plural in English – include examples of each.

4. Identify and classify the nouns in the following extract from a short story by Edgar Allan Poe:

   Approaching the table, I saw on it a large box, or case, nearly seven feet long, and perhaps three feet wide, by two and a half feet deep. It was oblong – not coffin-shaped. The material was at first supposed to be the wood of the sycamore (platanus), *but upon cutting into it, we found it to be pasteboard, or, more properly, papier mâché, composed of papyrus. It was thickly ornamented with paintings, representing funeral scenes, and other mournful subjects – interspersed among which, in every variety of position, were certain scenes of hieroglyphical characters, intended, no doubt, for the name of the departed. By good luck, Mr Gliddon formed one of our party; and he had no difficulty in translating the letters, which were simply phonetic, and represented the word,* Allamistakeo.

5. Identify and classify all the nouns in the following extract from *As I Walked Out One Midsummer Morning* by Laurie Lee:

   The morning came for departure, and the children helped me pack and Mike gave me his pocket jack-knife. Beth had gone off to work, leaving me a note of farewell, and Mrs Flynn was asleep. Patsy walked half way to the station with me, and we stopped on Putney Bridge. It was a fine chill morning, with a light mist on the river and the tide running fast to sea. Patsy stood on tip-toe and grabbed hold of my ear and pulled it down to her paint-smeared mouth. 'Take me with you,' she said, then gave a quick snort of laughter, waved goodbye, and ran back home.

The Apostrophe

The use of the apostrophe in English is much less complicated than people think. The apostrophe has two functions:

- to indicate that a letter is missing: *haven't, isn't, doesn't* (in each case the letter *o* is missing); *it's, everybody's here, the ruler's broken* (in each case the letter *i* is missing);

- to indicate possession – *the dog's blanket* (meaning the blanket belonging to the dog).

The rule for possession could not be easier:

- the apostrophe always comes before the *s*, except when the plural is formed by adding an *s*.

You now know that English forms the plural of nouns in a number of ways, but it is only when the plural is formed by adding an *-s* that the apostrophe come after the *s*:

SINGULAR – the apostrophe is always placed before the *s*		PLURAL when the plural is formed by adding an *s* or *es*	
bottle	bottle's	bottles	bottles'
dog	dog's	dogs	dogs'
lady	lady's	ladies	ladies'
SINGULAR – always before the *s*		PLURAL – the apostrophe goes before the *s* when the plural is formed by changing the vowel	
man	man's	men	men's
woman	woman's	women	women's
SINGULAR – the apostrophe is always before the *s*		PLURAL – before the *s* where the plural is formed by adding *en*	
child	child's	children	children's
ox	ox's	oxen	oxen's

Important

Where an awkward sound is created by too many double *s* sounds, then the apostrophe can go after the *s*:

Burns' songs.

Socrates' philosophy.

Moses' story.

Important Note

The simplest way of remembering how to use the apostrophe where it indicates possession:

- place the apostrophe after the *s* when the plural is formed by adding an *s*.
- If the plural is formed in any other way, the apostrophe is placed before the *s*.

Important Note

When a possession belongs to two or more people, the apostrophe is attached only to the last-named person. For example:

- I was invited to Sophie and Matthew's house.
- The teacher liked Mark and Alison's singing.

Quick Test 4

1. Rewrite these sentences using the apostrophe. The first one is done for you:
    - The coat belonging to the boy. – The boy's coat.
    - The scarf belonging to the girl.
    - The tickets belonging to the senior citizens.
    - The pullover belonging to the man.
    - The candy floss belonging to the children.
    - The cars belonging to the men.
    - The money belonging to the bank manager.
    - The dresses belonging to the ladies.
    - The ship belonging to the captain.
    - The ploughs belonging to the oxen.
    - The computer belonging to the mother.
    - The shoes belonging to the aliens.
    - The car belonging to Andrew and John.

2. The following sentences have mistakes with capital letters, plurals, apostrophes. Re-read the previous sections, then try to correct the mistakes.
    - Yesterday, I travelled to London to see downing street.
    - I'll meet you at the Train Station.
    - My favourite season is Summer, though I like spring when you see the Daffodils.
    - I took the train to Manchester to see united play city.
    - Thats my sons' tracksuit.
    - Never in my life have I seen such a mess by the Seaside.
    - That roofer has repaired over Fifteen rooves.
    - My cousin mary likes lamb for tea.
    - The ancient britons were of the scots and picts.

A pronoun is a word that substitutes for a noun or noun phrase. There are personal pronouns ('I, you, he/she/it, we and they'), possessive pronouns, reflexive and reciprocal pronouns, demonstrative pronouns, relative and interrogative pronouns, and indefinite pronouns.

Pronouns are used in place of nouns to avoid repetition. For example, take the sentences:

- John walked to the station where he caught the train into town. When he got on, he saw that it was very busy.

Now we'll remove the pronouns:

- John walked to the station where John caught the train into town. When John got on, John saw that the train was very busy.

In fact, without the pronouns, there is a lack of clarity – is the second John the same John as the first one? With pronouns, everything is much clearer – and the lack of repetition (three Johns and two trains) makes the sentence less clumsy.

With relative pronouns, use *who* when referring to a person or a pet; use *which* when referring to an animal; and use *that* when referring to an object. For example:

- John is the person who caught the train.

Because John is a person, you have to use *who* (note you DO NOT use *that* with a person, despite the recent fashion).

With animals use *which* or *that*, though if the animal is known to you, you would use *who*, otherwise *which* or *that*:

- My dog, Rover, who is four years old today got his favourite dinner.
- The tiger that escaped yesterday was eventually caught.

And *that* for inanimate objects:

- The table that I bought yesterday has a mark on the top.

The following table classifies pronouns. (Some comments refer to verbs – for more information about verbs see pages 29–32.)

Pronouns	Example of pronoun	Function
Personal pronouns	I, you (singular), he, she, it, we, you (plural), they. *He jumps, you draw, they swim.*	Used in place of the proper name of someone.
Personal pronouns	me, you, him, her, it, us, you (plural), them.	Used in place of a name, making clear who we are talking about.

Pronouns	Example of pronoun	Function
Possessive pronouns (before a noun)	my, your, his, her, its, our, your, their.	Indicates belonging – e.g. *my book, his bicycle* (note that the possessive 'its' does NOT have an apostrophe).
Possessive pronouns	mine, yours, his, hers, its, ours, yours, theirs.	Indicates belonging – e.g. *the book in mine, the bicycle is yours.*
Reflexive pronouns	myself, yourself, himself, herself, itself, ourselves, yourselves, themselves.	Used after a verb, – e.g. *I am washing myself.* Reflexive pronouns refer to the person already mentioned.
Relative pronouns	who, whom, whose, which, that, as.	Help join units of sense into one sentence. *That is the man **who** walked here; the woman **whose** house has been bought; here is the wall **that** has fallen down.*
Demonstrative pronouns (before a noun)	this, these, that, those.	Used to make clear what person or object is being referred to. *This book is valuable; that car is very modern.*
Interrogative pronoun (before a question)	who, what, which, what's, whose.	Used to ask questions. *Which came first? Whose book is that? What is the dog's name?*
Reciprocal pronouns	each other, one another.	Use *each other* when two people are involved in a reciprocal arrangement – e.g. *John and Jean talked to each other yesterday;* use *one another* when more than two people are involved – e.g. *the girls were talking to one another.*

Articles

You need to know the terms *definite* and *indefinite article*. You already know what they are – you just might not know these terms.

> The **definite article** is the word *the*
> The **indefinite articles** are the words *a* and *an*.

These articles function to make clear who or what we are talking about.

- *The* boy crossed *a* road.

The word *the* makes clear that we are talking about a specific boy and the word *a* indicates that it isn't any particular road.

Quick Test 5

1. Find a short piece from the Internet or a newspaper or magazine, copy it and identify all the pronouns you can find.
2. Find the definite and indefinite articles in the same piece.

By now you know about
personal, possessive, reflexive, relative, interrogative, demonstrative, and reciprocal pronouns, definite and indefinite articles.

Prepositions

Prepositions are words that indicate relationships between people and/or animals and/or objects. For example, between people:

- Mary is talking *to* Tom
- Alistair is *with* his parents.
- *Notwithstanding* the facts, the jury found the defendant guilty

Or between people/animals and objects:

- Morgan is sitting *at* his desk.
- Ahmed's feet are *under* the table.
- Rover is lying *in* his basket.
- Gavin always takes his dog *for* a walk.
- The rider was *astride* the horse.

Or between objects:

- The book is *in* the library.
- The newspaper is *on* the table.
- There is paper *in* the printer.
- The café is *opposite* the cinema.
- The house shook *during* the storm.
- There is a fish lying *among* the willowherbs.

Prepositional phrases

But prepositions can also be in the form of **prepositional phrases** – and you have to be able to recognise them. For example:

- I drove *down the motorway*.
- I delivered my talk *in front of the whole class*.
- There were *in excess of 10,000 people* who were *at the match*.
- We will travel *by the M74* when we are *on the way* south.
- Three people turned up *in addition to* those invited.
- *In the morning*, we cycled all the way north.

In any sentence, when you shift the position of a prepositional phrase, you change the meaning – usually by changing emphasis. Take the third sentence above as an example:

- There were *in excess of 10,000 people* who were *at the match*.

Here there are two prepositional phrases: *in excess of 10,000 people* and *at the match*. Now change the position of one of these prepositional phrases – and note the change as a result:

- *In excess of 10,000 people* were at the match.

The sentence is more direct, and the position of the prepositional phrase draws attention to the number of people involved.

Now let's take another example:

- I will talk to my teacher after school.

Change the position of the prepositional phrase:

- After school, I will talk to my teacher.

By shifting the prepositional phrase to the beginning of the sentence, you draw attention to it, thus emphasising it. The position of the phrase draws attention to *when* the boy will talk to his teacher.

Note also that when you place a prepositional phrase at the beginning of a sentence, you need a comma to separate the phrase from the rest of the sentence. Look at the fourth sentence above:

- We will travel *by the M74* when we are *on the way* south.

If you shift either or both of the prepositional phrases, you will alter the meaning.

- On the way south, we will travel by the M74.

By placing *On the way* south at the beginning of the sentence attention is drawn to the destination rather than the route but remember that it must be separated by a comma.

Quick Test 6

1. Identify the prepositional phrase(s) in the following sentences and try shifting their position – comment on the effect of the new position.
   - I talked to my teacher later in the day.
   - The asteroid missed the Earth by 50 kilometres.
   - I do my homework in the morning.
   - Mary began to like Scotland after a few years.
   - The committee meets in Holyrood every third week.

2. Using three examples, show that you know the function of prepositions.

By now you know about
- **nouns and their plurals**
- **apostrophes**
- **pronouns**
- **prepositions and prepositional phrases**
- **definite and indefinite articles**

Adjectives

Adjectives are often defined as 'describing words' and there are adjectives that describe things or people. Adjectives also describe quality, quantity, colour and number. The main function of adjectives is to describe or modify *a noun*. For example:

- It was an interesting TV series.

The adjective 'interesting' is describing the noun 'TV series', telling us what the TV series was like. But the adjective can also come after the noun:

- The TV series was interesting.

You can have a list of adjectives – as many as you like:

- The large, long-haired, scary, brown dog came running towards us.

There are four adjectives in that list, one of which is a compound adjective – 'long-haired'. Note that when there is a list of adjectives they have to be separated by commas.

Quick Test 7

1. Identify the adjectives in the following sentences:
   - You can climb that faraway hill by either route.
   - That poor young man has caught a nasty cold.
   - There were five green and blue glass beads on the pine table.
   - We met several different animals at the dried-out water hole.

Premodifiers

Premodifiers are adjectives that come before a noun and modify or describe the qualities of the noun or pronoun. The adjectives are in italics:

- That *beautiful*, *vibrant* painting.
- The *tall*, *elegant* stranger entered the *blue* room.
- The *thick*, *impenetrable* fog swirled round the *dilapidated*, *old*, *rickety* house.

These adjectives are in random order and commas are needed between each adjective.

On the other hand, sometimes the order isn't random. For example, colour adjectives need to be placed as close to the noun as possible and number adjectives as far from the noun as possible. For example:

- There are *ten green* bottles.

In this case commas aren't used because the adjectives are in a specific order.

> **Note:** colour adjectives are placed close to the noun they modify while number adjectives are placed as far as possible from the noun they modify.

Some examples:

- The red sun sank beneath the distant, dark horizon. *[commas needed because 'distant' and 'dark' are in random order and can be reversed]*
- There were fifteen Saturday players all dressed in the new blue strips. *[no commas needed because the order of the adjectives cannot be altered]* – to write: 'There were Saturday fifteen players all dressed in the blue new strips' would sound odd!

Another example:

- The clever, fast greyhound cleared the fence in one great leap.

Let's analyse the words:

The (definite article) *clever* (adjective) *fast* (adjective) *greyhound* (noun) *cleared* (verb) *the* (definite article) *fence* (noun) *in one great leap* (prepositional phrase).

Quick Test 8

Analyse the following sentences by classifying the words (as above):

   (i)   Cold snow-laden artic air causes blizzards throughout the north.
   (ii) There are many brilliant things happening across Scotland this winter!
       (*Scotrail advert*)

Postmodifiers

Postmodifiers, on the other hand, are adjectives that come after a linking verb – verbs such as *to be*, or *to feel, to seem, to live, to contain, to appear, to see, to hear, to touch, to taste, to smell*. In the following sentences, the post-modifier adjectives are in **bold**:

- That boy is **clever**.
- The car's exhaust seems **noisy**.
- The sea can be **cruel**.
- That fish tastes **oily**.
- She is **confident** and **clever**.

Quick Test 9

1.   Identify and classify the adjectives in the following sentences, making clear which are premodifiers and which are postmodifiers:

- The weather was wet and foggy that dreadful day.
- A lost treasure was found on the far side of the tropical island.
- That venerable old man spoke with a soft, lilting, mellifluous voice.
- After the race, Gordon had bright red cheeks and was happy.
- James had been unwell but has made a remarkable recovery.
- The 44-year-old, dark-haired, Giffnock housewife told our roving reporter…
- The big, old, expensive, Tudor mansion was burned to the ground.
- Hero pensioner rescues frightened tree-bound cat.

Comparison (or degrees) of adjectives

We often use adjectives to compare two or more people or items. For example, we can say that Connor is taller than Sam, where 'taller' is the comparative of the adjective 'tall'. If there are three of them – Connor, Sam and Hugh – we could say that one of them is the 'tallest'.

We refer to 'tall' as the adjective referred to here as the positive, 'taller' as the comparative and 'tallest' as the superlative. The superlative is used when there are more than two items/people being compared.

Positive

The positive is an adjective that simply and straightforwardly describes a noun or pronoun. For example, a *warm* sea, a *tall* plant, this cup is *broken*.

Comparative

The comparative is used when we compare a person, animal, thing or group with **one** other person, animal, thing or group. For example, Clara is *smaller* than her sister, Your cat is *greedier* than mine, Is the Caspian Sea *larger* than the Black Sea?

Superlative

The superlative is used when we compare a person, animal, thing or group with **more than one** other. For example, Bill is the tallest in the class, The Blue whale is the largest animal on Earth, Which is the longest river in Scotland?

Adjective (known as the positive)	Comparative (formed by adding -er when two items are being compared)	Superlative (formed by adding -est when more than two are being compared)
tall	taller	tallest
clever	cleverer	cleverest
blue	bluer	bluest
happy	happier	happiest

When it comes to words of **more than two syllables**, we have to use 'more' and 'most'. For example:

Adjective	Comparative (two items are being compared)	Superlative (more than two are being compared)
beautiful	more beautiful	most beautiful
difficult	more difficult	most difficult
expensive	more expensive	most expensive
authentic	more authentic	most authentic

There are also **some irregular ways of comparing matters**, which you just have to know:

Adjective	Comparative (when two items are being compared)	Superlative (when more than two are being compared)
good	better	best
bad	worse	worst
little	less	least
much	more	most
many	more	most
far	further	furthest

Quick Test 10

Write down the comparatives and superlatives of the following adjectives:
- Little, amazing, happy, fast, hideous, kind-hearted, bad, late.

By now you know about
Adjectives – that they describe or modify a noun;

premodification and postmodification;

comparison of adjectives.

Adverbs

An adverb is a word that modifies or gives us additional information about a verb, an adjective, another adverb or a word group. For example:

Alfred brushed his teeth carefully this morning.

The adverb 'carefully' tells us *how* Alfred brushed his teeth – he brushed them *carefully*. When the adverb tells us *how* something happened, it is referred to as an adverb of *manner*.

Adverbs indicate manner, time, place, cause, degree, circumstance, reason. Often, adverbs answer questions such as *how? where? why? when?*

The table below sets out types of adverbs and their functions. (Some comments refer to verbs – for more information about verbs see pages 29–32.)

Type of adverb	Answers the question –	Example	Comment
Place	Where?	Here, there, everywhere – For example, 'We'll all go *indoors*'.	The adverb 'indoors' modifies the verb 'to go' informing us where the people went – indoors.
Time	When?	Soon, then, now, before, later, first – For example, 'I shopped there *yesterday*'.	The adverb 'yesterday' tells us when the person shopped.
Manner	How?	She shouted so *loudly*!	'loudly' tells us how she shouted – note the intensifier 'so'.
Reason / cause / purpose	Why? / What caused it?	Because, therefore, hence – For example, '*Since* I was tired, I went to bed'.	'Since' indicates the reason that the writer went to bed.
Contrast / concession / condition	What are the opposites?	If, though, while, whereas, although – For example, '*Although* Penny has a degree, she works in Macdonald's'.	There is a contrast between having a degree and yet working in an unchallenging job.

Type of adverb	Answers the question –	Example	Comment
Degree	To what extent?	Really, honestly, absolutely, rather – For example, 'I am *absolutely* sure I've finished my essay'.	Adverbs of degree are used to show the intensity, degree, or extent of the verb they modify. They always appear before the verb. Here, the word 'absolutely' indicates the degree to which the person is sure that the essay has been finished; similar words – 'honestly', 'barely', 'deeply', 'so' (as in *so* good).
Affirmation	Before a verb	'He can *definitely* swim.'	'definitely' affirms the fact that he can swim.
Negation	Before a verb	'I have *never* been to Golspie.'	'never' indicates that the speaker has not been to Golspie. 'Not' is another adverb of negation.

Connectives/transition words

Conjunctions connect parts of sentences together to make one sentence – words such as 'and', 'or', 'but'. But adverbs can also be used to connect parts of sentences – for example, if you look again in the table above, you will see that words such as 'although', 'after', 'since', 'when' 'while', 'as' behave as adverbial connectives. You need to know about adverbial connectives in order to understand the effect of certain sentence structures (see pages 41–42).

When you conclude an essay, you probably use words such as 'In conclusion', 'to sum up', 'finally' – these are adverb connectives, linking your conclusion to the main part of your essay.

Quick Test 11

The object of this exercise is to see if you can tell the difference between adverbs and adverbial connectives.
Identify the connectives in the following sentences (the first two have been done for you):

- My friend studies hard, whereas I do very little. ('*whereas*' is an adverb sentence connective; '*hard*' and '*very little*' are adverbs)
- When I was in front of the camera, I could not stop laughing.
- Although I have sent her several texts, she still hasn't replied.
- Finally, the volcano erupted.
- Unless the team practises hard, they will never succeed.

Adverbial phrases

You'll have noticed that although adverbs can be one word – such as 'slowly', 'deliberately', 'gently' – others are in the form of phrases. Indeed, some are adverbial clauses (for information about clauses see pages 43–45).

Look at the following table:

	Sentence	Phrase(s)
1	John shouted defiantly.	The word *defiantly* is clearly an adverb – note that many adverbs end in -*ly*. The adverb 'defiantly' tells us *how* John shouted – it is therefore an adverb of manner.
2	Julie quickly entered the room.	The word *quickly* is an adverb but note that it can be placed before or after the verb (Julie entered the room quickly). The word *quickly* is an adverb of manner – answers the question *how*.
3	The cake was really tasty.	The word *really* is an adverb – again note that it ends in -*ly*. The adverb *really* indicates the degree of tastiness.
4	Karen drove down the motorway in the morning.	There are two adverbial phrases – *down the motorway* and *in the morning*. The first tells us *where* Karen drove and the second tells us *when* she did the driving.
5	The playground was empty because it was raining.	The phrase *because it was raining* is adverbial. This adverbial clase gives us the reason *why* the playground emptied.
6	If you stare at the shark, it won't attack you.	*If you stare at the shark* is an adverbial clause of condition. The phrase sets out the condition for not being attacked by the shark.

In the table above:

- sentence numbers 1–3 use *single adverbs* – 'defiantly', 'quickly', 'really';
- sentence number 4, on the other hand, uses *adverbial phrases* – 'down the motorway' and 'in the morning'; also note that this sentence begins with an adverbial phrase – 'on the other hand';
- sentences 5 and 6 use *adverbial clauses** – 'because it was raining' and 'If you stare at the shark'.

* You will learn about clauses on pages 43–45.

Quick Test 12

Read the following sentences carefully, then indicate the adverbs and/or adverbial phrases and also identify the type of adverb (as in the table above).

- In the eight years of living in London, I have never travelled south of the river.
- Suddenly, without lifting my head, I saw what had happened.
- Some batteries last for a long time.
- Some people feel marginalised, out on the edge of society.

Adverbs or adverbial phrases at the beginning of sentences

The placing of adverbs or adverbial phrases at the beginning of sentences is commoner than you might think – and can alter the meaning of the sentence.

You need to be aware of the normal order of an English sentence. Take the following sentence:

- The procession suddenly stopped short without any order or warning when we had gone ten yards.

It follows the normal order that you would expect. But you can detect that there are three adverbs/adverbial phrases in that sentence: *suddenly*, *without any order or warning*, and *when we had gone ten yards*. Now let's look at the actual sentence written by George Orwell in his essay, *A Hanging*:

- Suddenly, when we had gone ten yards, the procession stopped short without any order or warning.

By placing *suddenly* and *when we had gone ten yards* at the beginning of the sentence, Orwell breaks the normal word order – and gains a significant emphatic effect by drawing attention to the extent (degree) of speed at which they stopped (*suddenly*) and the time and place at which they stopped (*when we had gone ten yards*), thus emphasising the suddenness, the quickness and the location of the event that caused the procession to stop.

Adverbs can be in the form of prepositional phrases, again at the beginning of sentences: look out for 'In the first place', 'After that', 'Originally', 'Eventually' or such like at the beginning of sentences, drawing attention in these cases to time, but adverbs can be of place or manner (for example, 'Condescendingly, she allowed him to escort her to the prom...').

Quick Test 13

Read carefully the following sentences, then alter the word order by placing any adverbial phrases in a different, but appropriate, position in each sentence in order to alter meaning. Say in what way you have altered the meaning.

- I will be leading a walking African safari through the bush in five weeks' time.
- I always drive by car when I drive to Glasgow.
- I try to finish my homework early each evening as a rule.
- I sometimes let my head drop back when it is dark and look up at the clear sky.
- I've found a way of keeping on the move in the Duke of Edinburgh hill walk.

Intensifiers

Intensifiers are adverbs or adverbial phrases that strengthen the meaning of other expressions to show emphasis. They are a subset of adverbs of degree, The most common intensifiers include *very, totally, absolutely, completely, extremely, highly, rather, really, so* (as in *I am so excited*), *too, utterly,* and *at all*. Very often such adverbs/intensifiers modify an adjective. For example:

- There are some films which people find deeply disturbing.

Now although 'deeply' is an adverb, it is also highlighting and strengthening – intensifying – the extent to which people find some films disturbing – they find them intensely, profoundly distressing. And note that the adverb is intensifying the adjective *disturbing*.

Quick Test 14

In about 150 words, write a paragraph about a walk along a beach using as many intensifiers as you think appropriate.

Remember that adverbs are used more commonly than you may think.

They are used:

- to modify a verb or add to the meaning of a verb
- to modify an adjective
- to modify another adverb
- in the form of phrases and/or clauses (see pages 43–45)

Verbs

The verb is one of the main word classes in any language.

Verbs have five properties: tense, person, number, mood, voice.

We shall begin with the first three of these properties:

- tense (present, past, future)
- person (first [I, we], second [you], third [he, she, it, they])
- number (singular, plural)

Together, they allow us to **conjugate** a verb – that means to set out the different forms of a verb according to tense, person, number, mood (as indicated above).

When you identify tenses in English, you also need to consider person, and number.

Tense is the means by which we communicate time. We have past tense, present tense and future tense. Because we can go back in time and then further back in time, we have more than one past tense.

Look carefully at the table below. We begin with the present tense of the verb *to walk*. Note that we recognise verbs by their **infinitive**, where we use the word 'to' as in 'to walk, to jump, to drive'.

In the table you will see that when we deal with tense, we indicate person and number at the same time – singular and plural.

In English, there are three present tenses:

Simple present tense	Singular	Plural
First person	I walk	We walk
Second person	You walk	You walk
Third person	He/she/it walks	They walk

Continuous present tense	Singular	Plural
First person	I am walking	We are walking
Second person	You are walking	You are walking
Third person	He/she/it is walking	They are walking

Emphatic present tense	Singular	Plural
First person	I do walk	We do walk
Second person	You do walk	You do walk
Third Person	He/she/it do walk	They do walk

There are several past tenses, but we will begin with the three past tenses:

Simple past tense	Singular	Plural
First person	I ran	We ran
Second person	You ran	You ran
Third person	He/she/it ran	They ran

Continuous past tense	Singular	Plural
First person	I was running	We were running
Second person	You were running	You were running
Third person	He/she/it were running	They were running

Emphatic past tense	Singular	Plural
First person	I did walk	We did walk
Second person	You did walk	You did walk
Third Person	He/she/it did walk	They did walk

Additionally, there is what we call the **perfect tense,** denoting completed action:

Perfect tense	Singular	Plural
First person	I have walked	We have walked
Second person	You have walked	You have walked
Third Person	He/she/it have walked	They have walked

There is also a **continuous perfect tense**.

Continuous perfect tense	Singular	Plural
First person	I have been walking	We have walked
Second person	We have been walking	You have been walking
Third Person	He/she/it has been walking	They have been walking

There is the **Past perfect (Pluperfect) Tense,** which goes further back in the past:

Pluperfect tense	Singular	Plural
First person	I had walked	We had walked
Second person	You had walked	You had walked
Third Person	He/she/it had walked	They had walked

There is a **continuous pluperfect tense:**

Continuous pluperfect tense	Singular	Plural
First person	I had been walking	We had been walking
Second person	You had been walking	You had been walking
Third Person	He/she/it had been walking	They had been walking

Finally, we come to the **Future Tense:**

Simple future tense	Singular	Plural
First person	I shall walk	We shall walk
Second person	You will walk	You will walk
Third Person	He/she/it will walk	They will walk

The Future Perfect Tense:

Future perfect tense	Singular	Plural
First person	I shall have walked	We shall have walked
Second person	You will have walked	You will have walked
Third Person	He/she/it will have walked	They will have walked

Auxiliary verbs

To form other tenses, we have to use the auxiliary verbs *shall, will, have, do, be.*

The future tense needs the words will and shall: You will go to the cinema. The verb in this instance – will – is known as an auxiliary verb. We can also use the auxiliary verb shall as in I shall go to the prom.

The auxiliary verb to go can also be used to form the future tense, as in I am going to go to English next period. Although I am going is in the present tense and to go is the infinitive, nevertheless the verbs together indicate the future.

The sentence You will have noticed is composed of two auxiliary verbs: shall and to have + noticed.

All tenses allow us to express events in time. There is, however, a difference between I lived in Glasgow for a long time (simple past tense / action completed) and I have lived in Glasgow for a long time (perfect tense / action still continuing).

When we form past tenses, the main auxiliary verbs are the verbs *to be, to have* and *to do*. Therefore, when you look for a verb in a sentence make sure that you identify the auxiliary part of the verb as well. For example, in the sentence:

- Charlene had decided to bleach her hair blonde before she was given the hair dye.

When identifying a verb, make sure you underline the auxiliary part of the verb as well as the main part. Thus:

- Charlene <u>had decided</u> to bleach her hair blonde before she <u>was given</u> the hair dye.

Note the use of the auxiliary verbs *had* and *was*.

> Always pay attention to the auxiliary verbs and underline the auxiliary part as well as the main part of the verb.

Clauses

It is now time to explain in detail about clauses. But to understand what a clause consists of, first you need to know about **finite verbs**:

Finite (or main) verbs

You should be able to recognise the main part of a verb. A finite verb is a main verb, with all its parts. Finite verbs express tense. For example:

- The dog <u>wagged</u> his tail.
- When I <u>lived</u> in Aberdeen, I <u>would visit</u> the fish market to buy fresh fish.

In the first sentence, *wagged* is a finite verb.

In the second sentence, there are two finite verbs (*lived* and *would visit*). But since *to buy* is an infinitive it is therefore *not* a finite or main verb.

The **verb** is traditionally referred to as the 'doing word'. Look at the sentence below:

- The young girl ate the apple.

In that sentence, the verb is quite definitely the doing word: what did the girl **do**? – she **ate** the apple!

But sometimes a verb does not signal action: sometimes it signals a state of being or existence. Take the sentence:

- My house stands at the edge of town.

Clearly, the house isn't **doing** anything – it is just standing there. But *stands* is still a verb. In the sentence, *My hair is brown* the word *is* is still a verb – even although once again it isn't a 'doing word'.

Some verbs, then, are more verbs of **being** or **existing** than doing (sometimes referred to as static verbs) – but you'll get used to spotting all verbs.

Non-finite verbs

A **non-finite verb** is a verb form that **does not show tense**.

In other words, a non-finite verb is only part of a verb and will not tell you if a sentence is in the past tense, present tense, or future tense. A non-finite verb, then, is never the main verb in a sentence.

There are three types of non-finite verbs:

- the infinitive – for example, *to wash, to jump, to talk, to swim*
- the present participle – for example, *washing, jumping, talking, swimming*
- the past participle – for example, *washed, jumped, talked, swam*

Quick Test 15

Read carefully the following sentences and list the finite verbs and identify the tense in each case:

- I wish I had finished all my homework.
- The dog swam across the river very slowly.
- Wendy jumped on the tram while eating her apple.
- The ship with the broken rudder sank slowly in the harbour.
- I am writing an essay for my teacher to mark.

Regular and irregular verbs

Regular verbs form the past tense and the past participle by adding *-ed*. For example:

Verb	Past tense	Past participle
To walk	walked	walked
To smile	smiled	smiled
To dance	danced	danced

Irregular verbs, on the other hand, form the past tense and the past participle in three different ways:

(i) Some irregular verbs make no change – all three forms remain the same:

Verb	Past tense	Past participle
To put	put	put
To read	read	read
To broadcast	broadcast	broadcast

(ii) Some have two forms that remain the same:

Verb	Past tense	Past participle
To sit	sat	Sat
To lead	led	Led

(Please note the spelling of the past tense and past participle of *led*)

(iii) Some have three different forms:

Verb	Past tense	Past participle
To drink	I drank	I have drunk
To sing	sang	sung
To swim	swam	swum
To do	did	done

We have looked at tense, person and number. Now we need to look at mood and voice.

Modal verbs

As well as auxiliary verbs (*to be*, *to have*, and *to do*), English also uses **modal verbs**. Modal verbs indicate mood, such as likelihood or permission or suggestion or possibility or necessity or obligation. The most common modal verbs are:

can, could, should, would, may, might, shall, will, ought to, must

You should (note my use of the modal verb *should*) note these characteristics of modal verbs:

- They do not have an infinitive – you can't say, for example, *to can*.
- They are, however, followed by an infinitive of another verb BUT without the *to*. For example, *You shall go on holiday*, where the *to* from *to go* has been dropped.
- There is no -*s* in the third person singular. For example, you can't say *he mights*.

Voice

In English, there are two voices – active and passive.

In the active voice, the subject of the sentence is the person who does the action. When we want to draw attention to the doer of the action, we use the active voice. For example:

The dog bit the man.

The dog is the one who did the biting.

When we want to draw attention to the action rather than the doer of the action, we use the passive voice. In the passive voice, the subject of the verb is NOT performing the action. For example:

The man was bitten by the dog.

The passive voice is used in more formal English. For example:

It was decided by the committee decided that no further decision could be taken at this time.

Phrasal verbs

English also has a number of phrasal verbs. Such verbs are made up of a verb of movement and a preposition – for example: *pick up, work out, put off, jump down, put out, stand up.*

Famously, the following line from *Othello* by William Shakespeare uses a phrasal verb, which gets repeated:

- *Put out* the light, and then *put out* the light.

The repetition of the phrasal verb *Put out* draws attention to Othello's action in extinguishing the candle and then Desdemona's life.

Quick Test 16

1. Read carefully the following sentences and note the modal verbs in each case:
   - I really should finish all my homework.
   - The dog must swim across the river very slowly.
   - Wendy ought not to jump on the tram while eating her apple.
2. Read carefully the following sentences and say which are in the active voice and which in the passive voice:
   - The girls should really see their mother.
   - The window was broken by the man.
   - The whole area was flooded by the rising tide.

Inflection

Many languages – French, German, Italian, Spanish – are *inflected* languages – that is meaning is determined by the ending of a word.

Inflection is where a word is modified, mainly by altering a word ending, to indicate different grammatical functions such as tense, case, voice, person, number, gender, mood.

In English, we have lost most inflections, though we indicate the third person singular of verbs by adding 's' or 'es': for example, 'he goes', 'she listens', 'the dog begs', 'the teacher does'. We also add -ed to form the simple past tense (for example, *jumped, crossed*) and -*ing* to form the present participle (for example, *walking, jumping, living*). Also the present tense of the verb *to be* has inflections in the present singular, not by adding letters to the stock word, but by altering the stock word:

Singular	Plural
I am	we are
you are	you are
he/she/it is	they are

In the past tense, the second person singular and the plural are altered:

Singular	Plural
I was	we were
you were	you were
he/she/it was	they were

Other languages are much more inflected and often form various tenses by adding letters. We can make this clear using the French verb *parler (to talk)*:

First person singular – present tense	First person singular – future tense
Je parle	Je parlerai

Note that French indicates the future tense by modifying the present tense *parle* to *parlerai*. English can't form the future tense by inflecting the stock word, therefore we have to add the auxiliary words *will* or *shall*.

First person singular – present tense	First person singular – future tense
I talk	I shall talk

Most languages are inflected languages – they modify words to form different grammatical functions. English has very few inflections – mainly the first person singular, where we add an *s* (he/she/it talks) or an *es* (he/she/it does).

Quick Test 17

Explain the difference in meaning between:
- I shall be living in Kirkcaldy *and* I should have been living in Kirkcaldy.
- I lived in St Andrews *and* I am living in St Andrews.
- I shall live in Stornoway *and* I shall have been living in Stornoway.
- I should have been living in Dunfermline *and* I was living in Dunfermline.

Minor sentences and conditional tense

Minor or verbless sentences

Occasionally, you find a sentence that doesn't have a verb. Such sentences are referred to as verbless sentences or minor sentences.

The following are the first lines of Carol Ann Duffy's poem *Stealing*. The minor sentences have been underlined:

Stealing

The most unusual thing I ever stole? <u>A snowman</u>.

<u>Midnight</u>. He looked magnificent; a tall, white mute

beneath the winter moon.

There are two minor sentences – *A snowman.* and *Midnight.*

- I saw her. Eating an apple.

The present participle (in this case *eating*) is not a main/finite verb, therefore the sentence – *Eating an apple* – is a minor sentence.

> ### Quick Test 18
>
> Write a paragraph (250 words) about getting up in the morning. Try to use as many minor sentences as you can. The following is a possible beginning (but try to create your own).
>
> **Now? She says I have to get up. Now! Just five more minutes! Easy. Back to sleep. Doze.**

Not all of these short sentences are minor sentences. 'Doze.' for example is a verb, therefore not a minor sentence. Try to capture how you are in the morning to make your writing interesting.

Conditional tense

English also has a conditional tense: for example, where 'if x' is a condition that has been met, then 'y' will follow in the future. This applies when we are sure of the result of the condition. For example:

- If she doesn't work hard, she will fail her exams.

By not working hard, it is fairly certain that she will fail, therefore we can use the simple future tense. Again:

- If I speak nicely to my mum, she will take me to the cinema.
- If it gets cold, I shall turn the heating up.
- If the car breaks down, we will have to take the train.

You can of course reverse the order and have the conditional following:

- I shall turn the heating on if it gets cold.
- We will have to take the train if the car breaks down.

But sometimes, we are not so certain about the outcome of the condition, in which case we use the words *might, may, could, would.* For example:

- If I the weather improves later, I might go for a walk.
- If I could save more money, I could buy a new phone.
- Unless I wear uniform, I won't be allowed on the school trip.
- If I were you, I would tell the teacher the truth. (Note the use of 'were')

Important Note

Remember that there are (at least) two parts to a conditional sentence:

(a) the condition, usually beginning with *If, unless, If I / he / she / it were*; and

(b) the outcome (or possible outcome) if the condition is met.

If you check back to pages 26, you will see that conditional clauses are adverbial. (Note: that sentence contains a conditional clause!)

Quick Test 19

1. Identify the tense in the following sentences:
    - I have been swimming all morning.
    - I learned some French verbs today.
    - I am going to the cinema next Tuesday.
    - By the time I get to Aberdeen, I will have been travelling for three hours.
    - I have been going to Paris for years now.
2. In about 250 words, write a story from first person point of view in the present tense where the writer looks back on a past event.
3. Answer the following questions:
    - What are the five properties of verbs?
    - What is a phrasal verb? Give an example.
    - What is meant by a conditional sentence? Give an example.
    - What is a verbless/minor sentence? Give an example.
    - What is an auxiliary verb? Give an example.

Sentence structure

You now know about nouns, pronouns, adjectives, adverbs, and verbs – but how are all these put together to form a sentence?

Sentences are made up of clauses, which in turn are made up of groups of words, each of which are made up of individual words.

Take the sentence:

- The girl ate the apple.

You can easily recognise the verb (V) – 'ate' – but what about the other parts of that sentence? It is made up of a subject and an object. In this sentence, the answer to the question 'who ate?' is 'the girl' ate the apple, therefore 'the girl' is the subject (S) of the verb. We'll use the letter V to label the verb and S to label the subject:

```
     S        V
```
- The girl | ate | the apple.

The object complement

In the above example, we can ask – 'ate what?' And the answer is 'the apple', therefore 'the apple' is the object complement (O) of the verb. It *completes* the action of the verb. We'll refer to object complements as **O**:

```
     S        V        O
```
- The girl | ate | the apple.

If there isn't an answer to the question 'what?' of the verb, then there isn't an object complement. For example:

- The teacher appeared at the door.

The question 'appeared what?' does not make sense! Therefore there isn't an object. Such verbs are called 'intransitive' – verbs which do not take objects. Verbs such as to appear, to arrive, to belong, to exist, to fall, to laugh are intransitive, they never take objects.

Adjuncts

But what about the phrase 'at the door'? What part of the sentence does that phrase form? Such phrases (or word groups) are referred to as 'adjuncts' (A):

```
      S           V           A
```
- The teacher | appeared | at the door.

Any part of a sentence that isn't an S, V or O is an adjunct. Here are some examples:

```
      S         V          A
```
- The tram | arrived | at the platform.

```
              S        V        O        A
```
- The dog | ate his | food | hungrily.

```
               S          V                O                    A
```
- The yacht | crossed | the finishing line | yesterday.

The normal order of sentences in English is, then, S V O A.

We can alter that normal word order by shifting the A to a different position. In that last sentence above, we'll shift 'yesterday' to the beginning of the sentence:

- Yesterday, the yacht crossed the finishing line.

By placing the adjunct at the beginning of the sentence, we highlight *when* the yacht crossed the finishing line. You have already tried placing adverbs in different positions on page 27, but now you understand in more depth how rearranging sentence order can create effects.

Let's add another adverbial phrase to the sentence above:

```
              S          V               O                    A                    A
```
- The yacht | crossed | the finishing line | in the championship | yesterday.

There are now two adjuncts, either or both of which can be moved for effect:

- In the championships, yesterday, the yacht crossed the finishing line.

By placing the adjuncts at the beginning of the sentence, the writer draws attention to *where* and *when* the yacht crossed the finishing line. But also note the use of commas to indicate that normal word order has been altered.

Clauses

A clause is the basic part of most sentences: all clauses contain a main verb and a subject. (There are, however, minor sentences that do not contain a main verb – see page 39).

There are two types of clauses:

- main (or principal) clauses and
- subordinate (or dependent) clauses.

Both types must have a main verb, and since one verb represents one clause, two main verbs mean two clauses, and so on. (You learned about main verbs on pages 29-31.)

Main clauses

Let's examine the following sentence:

- The dog jumped over the burn.

In the above example, *jumped* is the main verb, therefore the sentence comprises one clause. It is a main clause because it stands by itself and makes sense: it isn't dependent on any other clauses.

Quick Test 20

Try finding the main verbs in the following sentences:
- The ship sailed into the harbour.
- A clause always contains a main verb.
- I buy my books online.
- Katy really likes fast cars.
- I never use my phone in school.

But not all parts of a verb make up a main verb: the infinitive, remember, doesn't count as a main verb. The infinitive is that part of the verb with *to* in front of it: *to speak*, *to run*, *to jump*, *to swim*.

Take the sentence:

- I like to run every morning.

The main verb is *like*. Since *to run* is the infinitive, it doesn't count as a main verb, therefore there is only one clause.

Quick Test 21

1. In the following sentences, spot the infinitive – but be careful:
    *   The captain indicated that his ship was ready to sail.
    *   Harry wants to go to the cinema tonight.
    *   Joe ate his breakfast quickly in order not to be late.
    *   I am going to go to the shops later.
    *   Ailsa began to walk down the path to the sea.

There are also other parts of the verb that don't make up a main verb – those parts that end in -*ing*, such as *walking, jumping, swimming, gardening, writing*. These are known as present participles.

*   Harry walked to school eating an apple.

The present participle *eating* is NOT a main verb. There is only one main verb in that sentence: *walked*. The sentence is made up, then, of only one clause.

Quick Test 21 continued

2. Now identify the main verbs in the following sentences:
    *   Sue decided to give Tom an apple before he ate his dinner.
    *   Alistair wanted to go swimming every morning.
    *   When he comes out of the pool, Alistair likes to go home eating an orange.
    *   Andrew gave Angela a slice of his pizza before going to bed.
    *   Alison goes to the cinema following the same route every Friday to see the latest films.

Remember
The clause is the basic structure of a sentence.

Subordinate or dependent clauses

You know about the main clause, but what is a subordinate clause? A subordinate clause is, as the name suggests, subordinate to or dependent on a main clause. (For the sake of consistency, we will refer to these clauses as subordinate clauses.)

Read the following sentence carefully:

The dog jumped over the burn which flowed through the garden.

In that sentence there are two main verbs: *jumped* and *flowed*, therefore there are two clauses. Let's use an upright stroke to separate the clauses:

The dog jumped over the burn | which flowed through the garden.

We know that the clause *The dog jumped over the burn* is a main clause because it can stand on its own and make sense, but the second clause – *which flowed through the garden* – makes no sense on its own. Try saying it aloud. Say it to someone else and that person will look puzzled. It is therefore a subordinate clause; it needs a main clause in order to make sense.

We'll label the main clause MC and the subordinate clause SC:

      MC   SC

The dog jumped over the burn | which flowed through the garden.

Another example:

The ship <u>sank</u> in the harbour | after it <u>had been struck</u> by a submarine.

There are two main verbs, therefore two clauses: *The ship sank in the harbour* (main clause) and *after it had been struck by a submarine* (subordinate clause).

We can set the sentence out thus:

      MC   SC

The ship sank in the harbour | after it had been struck by a submarine.

Quick Test 22

Using vertical lines, separate the main clause from the subordinate clauses in the following sentences:

- The tide started to flow as I was walking along the beach.
- When the afternoon began, I decided to go out for a walk.
- Eating an apple, I stood on the platform waiting for my train, which was already an hour late.
- I know that you are very clever.
- The ship heaved on the violent waves which at times were ten metres high.

More on sentences

A sentence can consist of a main clause and/or subordinate clauses or no clause at all.

Syntax

There are five types of syntax, that is of grammatically recognisable sentences:

- Simple sentences
- Compound sentences
- Complex sentences
- Compound-complex sentences
- Minor sentences

Syntax is the set of rules that creates a recognisable sentence.

Simple sentence [one main clause]:

- Mary climbed Ben Nevis yesterday.
- I get bored washing dishes.

Compound sentence [two (or more) main clauses joined by a conjunction, shown in bold]:

- Mary had a little lamb, **and** Robin had a goat.
- Mum likes tv, **but** my sister prefers the cinema.
- The couple ran down the stairs, **because** they could smell smoke.
- We may walk home, **or** we may take the late-night bus.
- I get bored watching television, **yet** I enjoy the cinema.

Note: Where there are two main clauses, each of which can stand alone, you need a comma before the co-ordinating conjunction – as above.

Compound sentence without a comma:

- Joanna went to the shops and bought bananas.
- The ship sailed into the harbour and berthed perfectly.
- Mary had a little lamb and kept it as a pet.

If the second clause does not have a subject, then no comma is needed.

Compound sentence [without conjunctions, joined by a semi-colon]:

- Alistair is going to the gym; he says he will be there all day.
- It began to snow yesterday; it is still snowing today.
- John cycles to school; Fred walks.

- Alison loves reading books; however, she finds film versions boring.

Complex sentence [a main clause and one (or more) subordinate clause(s)]:

- My dog barks when someone knocks on the door.

Compound-complex sentence [two or more main clauses and at least one subordinate clause]:

- When I arrive at school, even if I am late, I go to registration, and I sign in.
- I use a calculator, and I always get the right answer, especially for difficult sums, although my teacher disapproves.
- Martin always goes swimming in the afternoon, and he swims as far as the headland, even if the waves are quite high.

Minor sentence [any sentence that does not contain a finite verb]:

- A bat? Yes. Well? Bam! Another? No!

Forms of sentences

Sentences can take four forms:

- Statement   –   (I walk)
- Interrogative –   (Do I walk?)
- Imperative   –   (Walk!)
- Interjection   –   (Gosh! Aw!)

Let's find out more about *statements*.

You need to know about declarative sentences, which, as the name suggests, declare something. Declarative sentences are simple sentences and make an assertion. For example, 'I am going to say something to her when she gets home'.

You need to be able to recognise the following types of sentences:

A *declarative* sentence makes a statement, states a fact, an arrangement or an opinion.

- Goldilocks is a naughty young hooligan.

An *interrogative* sentence asks a question and is followed by a question mark.

- Is Goldilocks a thief?

An *imperative* sentence gives an instruction or a command. There is no subject as the subject is implied. Often the command ends with an exclamation mark.

- Do not steal porridge!

An *exclamatory* sentence expresses emphasis and is usually followed by an exclamation mark. Such sentences usually express strong emotions or opinions.

- I can't believe Goldilocks is a thief!
- That's scary!
- He is a wonderful artist!

Exclamatory sentences are not part of formal English (see pages 77–79). They often appear in emails or texts.

It is important to learn how to analyse sentence structure. You now know how sentences are put together – that is, you know about the grammar of the language – but now you need to use that knowledge to analyse the ways in which sentences are put together.

Moving the subordinate clause

Look at the following sentence:

       MC   SC

I always turn off my phone | when I arrive at school.

Now let's move the subordinate clause to the beginning of the sentence:

      SC   MC

When I arrive at school, | I always turn off my phone.

Because we have altered the normal word order of the sentence – by *inverting* the clauses – we have altered the meaning. The writer is now stressing, drawing attention to, *when* and *where* the phone is turned off.

Let's look at more examples.

           MC   SC

- There was a red car with its roof down | even although it was raining.

The sentence is in normal order, but we can move the subordinate clause to the beginning of the sentence, thus changing the effect:

        SC   MC

- Even although it was raining, | there was a red car with its roof down.

Because the sentence now highlights the fact that it was raining, the effect is to suggest surprise that the car was being driven with its roof down. When you move the subordinate clause to the beginning of the sentence you need to insert a comma after it – as above.

> Knowledge about basic grammar will keep your writing free from grammatical error and will also make answering questions about sentence structure much easier.

1. Look at the following extract from *Of Mice and Men* by John Steinbeck. It is the very first paragraph of the novel:

> A few miles south of Soledad, the Salinas River drops in close to the hillside bank and runs deep and green. The water is warm too, for it has slipped twinkling over the yellow sands in the sunlight before reaching the narrow pool. On one side of the river the golden foothill slopes curve up to the strong and rocky Gabilan mountains, but on the valley side the water is lined with trees.

   (a) Take each sentence in turn and indicate, using vertical parallel lines, the main clauses and any subordinate clauses.

   (b) Indicate the kind of sentences each one is: simple, compound, complex, compound-complex?

   (c) Pick out examples of adverbial phrases at the beginning of sentences. What do you think is the effect of Steinbeck's use of such adverbial phrases?

2. Write down a simple sentence, a compound sentence, and a compound-complex sentence.

3. Read again the second sentence of the extract and indicate, using vertical lines, the subject, verb, object, and adjuncts.

Meaning

Let's say some more about meaning in English. As you now know, English is a word ordered language – that is, meaning in English is dependent on the order of words in a sentence and not on word endings (inflection). Take the following sentence:

Alison loves Andrew.

Now let's alter the word order:

Andrew loves Alison.

Do these two sentences mean the same thing?

It's even more obvious in this example if we move –

Kevin loves tennis to *Tennis loves Kevin*

Meaning, in English, depends on word order, therefore if you alter the order of words, you alter the meaning. When you move a subordinate clause you alter meaning.

Defining clauses

Relative pronouns (*who, whom, which, that, whose*) can introduce relative clauses, which add description or give additional information. Sometimes, they are referred to as *adjective clauses* because they describe or modify a noun or a noun phrase. For example:

- Kevin sat on a rock which was right by the sea.

The clause *which was right by the sea* describes the rock, thereby defining it, making clear which rock Kevin sat on. The relative clause defines the rock.

A defining clause makes clear who or what is being referred to by giving essential information about that someone or something. Such a clause does NOT require commas. For example:

- Andrew who lives next door to me goes riding every Saturday.

The expression *who lives next door to me* doesn't require commas because it is defining which Andrew, out of lots and lots of Andrews. We are talking about the one who lives next door. Similarly:

- That's the boy who leant me his phone.

The expression *who leant me his phone* defines which boy we are talking about, so no commas.

Non-defining clauses

If it is clear who we are talking about, then the clause merely says something about the person or object and does require commas:

- The Queen, who is at Balmoral every August, loves to go for picnics.

The expression *who is at Balmoral every August* doesn't define which queen we are talking about – it merely gives us extra information about the Queen.

Analysis

Inversion

How to analyse sentence structure types

It is quite usual in both N5 and Higher courses to be asked about language analysis. You already know quite a bit about sentence structure, but you need to be able to recognise various sentence structure types. We shall go through them one by one.

There are several types of sentence structure that you need to know about, and you will find out how to analyse them all. We shall look at the way writers use inversion, lists, repetition, tenses, short sentences, and questions/imperatives.

Sometimes inversion involves only one word being shifted. The following sentence follows the 'normal' word order in English:

- Jason crossed the river slowly in his boat.

Sometimes, for emphasis, a writer changes the word order, by repositioning some of the words, even if it is just one word:

- Slowly, Jason crossed the river in his boat.

By placing 'Slowly' at the beginning of the sentence the writer draws attention to it, thereby emphasising *how* Jason crossed the river. But the phrase 'in his boat' can also be moved:

- In his boat, Jason crossed the river slowly.

Or even:

- In his boat, slowly, Jason crossed the river.

Words, especially adverbs, placed at the beginning of a sentence can draw attention to the importance of time, place, and manner.

The following extract, from a book by Gerrit L Verschuur called 'Impact! The threat of Comets and Asteroids', discusses the role of meteors in the formation of the Earth. Note how the writer uses adverbs and adverbial phrases at the beginning of each sentence:

Originally, such objects smashed into one another to build the earth 4.5 million years ago. After that, further comet impacts brought the water of our oceans and the organic molecules needed for life. Ever since then, impacts have continued to punctuate the story of evolution. On many occasions, comets slammed into earth with such violence that they nearly precipitated the extinction of all life. In the aftermath of each catastrophe, new species emerged to take the place of those that had been wiped out.

(i)   Write down the adverbs and adverbial phrases at the beginning of each sentence.

(ii) Comment on what kind of adverbs they are.

(iii) Comment on the cumulative effect of the adverbs.

In each of the examples above, by placing adverbial phrases at the beginning of the sentences, the normal word order has been altered. [Note the adverbial phrases at the beginning of that sentence!]

The normal word order of a complex sentence is when the main clause comes at the beginning of the sentence. For example:

- We are watching the harbour very carefully since it looks as though a storm is brewing.

Now we'll move the subordinate clause to the beginning of the sentence:

- Since it looks as though a storm is brewing, we are watching the harbour very carefully.

By shifting the subordinate clause – 'Since it looks as though a storm is brewing' – to the beginning of the sentence the writer is drawing attention to the reason that the harbour is being watched.

Inversion is when the subordinate clause is moved to the beginning of a sentence.

If you are asked about the effect of sentence structure, look for any uses of inversion.

Read the following paragraph from an article by John Cooper and Hannah Greig in 'History Extra':

> When the gunpowder plot was discovered, Londoners were encouraged to light bonfires in celebration. Before long, 5 November had entered the calendar as a reminder of England's deliverance. Mingling with the older traditions of fire-making and feasting, it became a day of national rejoicing.

(i) Indicate, by referring to each sentence, which part has been inverted.
(ii) In each case, say what is the effect of the inversion.

The following complex sentence is in normal order:

- Goldilocks heated her porridge in the microwave because it was cold.

Now we'll place the dependent clause at the beginning of the sentence:

- Because her porridge was cold, Goldilocks heated it in the microwave.

It isn't enough just to be able to spot inversion, you have to comment on its effect. In this case, the inversion draws attention to the reason for Goldilocks using the microwave, drawing attention to the coldness of the porridge.

> Remember
>
> There needs to be a comma after any word/phrase/clause that has been placed out of normal order.

Here is another example of inversion:

Jack always felt happy whenever he was at the seaside.

Now the inverted structure:

Whenever he was at the seaside, Jack always felt happy.

What is the effect of the inversion?

1. Invert the following sentences by moving the subordinate clause:
   - I poured my coffee away because it was too cold.
   - Darren was still unhappy although he was astonishingly wealthy.
   - She returned the computer after she noticed it was damaged.
2. In each case say what is the effect of the inversion.
3. Read the following paragraph carefully and return each sentence to normal word order:

When I arrived at the station, I could see from the electronic departure sign that the train was running over 30 minutes late. In the middle of the afternoon, what was I to do? Clearly, there was nowhere to buy a newspaper. From what I could see the train wasn't going to be busy. While I waited on the platform, I became aware of a commotion coming from the road below.

Write down three sentences showing that you understand inversion.

Climax

More often than you would realise, sentences are structured so that there is a build-up of increasing intensity till the main point at the end is highlighted – this structure is referred to as climax. There are various ways in which climax can be created, and most of them require words or phrases or clauses that create a delay thereby building up tension:

"Look! Up in the sky! It's a bird! It's a plane! It's Superman!"

Here the build-up is obvious – the repetition of 'It's a' contributes to the accumulation of terms for the flying object – from the size of a bird, increasing to a plane, then to the exciting climactic point of 'Superman'.

> Anaphora is the repetition of words or phrases at the beginning of clauses, but more of that on pages 61-62.

Climax draws attention to and highlights the point being made. To analyse climax, quote the climactic point, say what the point actually is and say how the climax draws attention to the point. Look out for and mention the use of phrases within the sentence to delay the main point to the end – thus reinforcing **climax**.

Climax also contributes to rhythm, thus making the sentence more memorable – readers remember the dramatic final point.

> Later in the day, after Little Red Riding Hood had finished the sandwiches that her grandmother had made for her, she went into the bedroom, smiled sweetly at what she knew was a wolf, pulled her beretta from her Louis Vuitton handbag and shot him dead.

This sentence has a long build-up – look at the phrases used to delay the main point right to the end. The climax highlights the surprise – that Little Red Riding Hood, not as innocent and vulnerable as she is presented in the folk story, gets the better of the big bad wolf.

Here is an extract from an essay by George Orwell, called *Marrakech*. Orwell is commenting on the poverty of people in 1930s Marrakech, and here he has come across a carpenter working at his lathe:

> He works the lathe with a bow in his right hand and guides the chisel with his left foot, and thanks to a lifetime of sitting in this position his left leg is warped out of shape. At his side, his grandson, aged six, is already starting on the simpler parts of the job.

Both sentences are climactic: in the first one the phrases 'with a bow in his right hand' and 'chisel in his left foot', as well as 'a lifetime of sitting in this position', all delay the main point about his left leg being warped out of shape till the end, thus highlighting the appalling effect of the cramped conditions on this man's limb.

The second sentence, revealing that the small grandson will end up as crippled as his grandfather, is clearly climactic. The phrases 'at his side', 'his grandson' and 'aged six' delay the main, profoundly serious point, that the child is going to be afflicted as well.

But the second sentence itself forms a climax to the whole paragraph, making clear that such poverty – and consequent disablement – will afflict generations of people.

Sometimes, a writer creates a list to build up to the final dramatic impact, emphasised by its position as the last item in the list.

Quick Test 27

The extract below, from Robert Louis Stevenson's *Treasure Island*, describes Jim Hawkins' reaction Billy Bones collapse after he had been given the black spot by Blind Pew:

The captain had been struck dead by thundering apoplexy. It is a curious thing to understand, for I had certainly never liked the man, though of late I had begun to pity him, but as soon as I saw that he was dead, I burst into a flood of tears. It was the second death I had known, and the sorrow of the first was still fresh in my heart.

1. Explain the effect of climax in these three sentences.
2. Explain how the climax was delayed in the second sentence.
3. Write a paragraph about a walk through woods where you use climax in at least three of you sentences.

Lists

One important aspect of sentence structure is the use of lists, a writing technique that illustrates the range (variety) and extent (amount) of whatever point the writer is making. It is not enough to identify a list, you must analyse the effect, which means showing how the range and extent of the items illustrate/highlight the point being made.

The following sentence is from an article by Steve Connor in *The Independent*. He is discussing the intelligence of chimpanzees in comparison to humans.

Chimpanzees make simple tools, they are fascinated by fire and rain and have even been known to appreciate a sunset.

The sentence is in the form of a list with three items – 'simple tools', 'fascinated by fire and rain', and 'known to appreciate a sunset'. You will be given credit for spotting the list, but you also have to comment on its effect. The writer is saying that chimpanzees are like humans and the list illustrates the variety and extent of activities which are human-like.

Quick Test 28

1. Read the following sentence taken from the same article:

They mourn their dead, they make war on members of the same species and, rather chillingly, they are said to be the only animal other than humans who deliberately plan the murder of rivals.

   (i) Identify the items that form a list.
   (ii) Comment on the effect of including these items.

2. The following sentence is taken from an article by Edward Collier in *The Guardian*.

Like good dog owners, we gave her doggy chews, all contemptuously ignored in favour of the TV remote, several telephones and the iron.

   (i) Identify the list in the sentence.
   (ii) Comment on the effect of the list.

3. From the same article:

She's very affectionate with a sweet nature, doesn't bark, puts up with our youngest son's brand of tough love and doesn't cost too much to run.

   (i) Again, identify the list in the sentence.
   (ii) Comment on the effect of the list.

Lists are used frequently by writers because they can convey so much so quickly to illustrate the point being made.

This scene by the author, Laurie Lee, from his autobiography, *Cider with Rosie*, describes his experience during his first day at school. Note Lee's use of lists.

The extract is from Chapter 3:

> I arrived at the school just three feet tall and fatly wrapped in my scarves. The playground roared like a rodeo, and the potato burned through my thigh. Old boots, ragged stockings, torn trousers and skirts, went skating and skidding around me. The rabble closed in; I was encircled; grit flew in my face like shrapnel. Tall girls with frizzled hair, and huge boys with sharp elbows, began to prod me with hideous interest. They plucked at my scarves, spun me round like a top, screwed my nose, and stole my potato.
>
> I was rescued at the last by a gracious lady – the sixteen-year-old junior-teacher – who boxed a few ears and dried my face and led me off to The Infants. I spent that first day picking holes in paper, then went home in a smouldering temper.

Look at the fourth sentence:

Old boots, ragged stockings, torn trousers and skirts, went skating and skidding around me.

You could argue that, in the above sentence, there are actually three sets of lists:

- list 1 containing three items: *Old boots, ragged stockings, torn trousers and skirts*;
- list 2, the third item in list 1, containing two items: (a) *torn trousers* and (torn) *skirts*; and
- list 3 containing two items: *skating and skidding*.

(See page 62 – tricolon – for lists with three items)

You must consider the effect of any sentence structure technique. Lists can have several different effects: look for the range (variety) and extent (amount) of whatever point is being made.

In the first list in this sentence, Lee conveys the range and extent of the old, worn clothes that these young pupils were wearing as well as the range – from 'Old boots' to 'torn skirts'. In the second list – 'skating and skidding' – Lee creates the feeling of movement as well as the range of activities by the pupils taking place near him.

> Remember that lists tend to illustrate / capture / demonstrate the range (variety) and extent (amount) of the subject being talked about. They can also use rhythm to create an emotional response from the reader.

Quick Test 28 continued

4. Read the following extract from *A Portrait of the Artist as a Young Man* by James Joyce: it describes Christmas in Ireland:

... the warm heavy smell of turkey and ham and celery rose from the plates and dishes and the great fire was banked high and red in the grate and the green ivy and red holly made you feel so happy and when dinner was ended the big plum pudding would be carried in, studded with peeled almonds and sprigs of holly, with bluish fire running around it and a little green flag flying from the top.

(i) Identify as many lists as you can.
(ii) Choose two of the lists you have identified and comment on the effect of the items in them.
(iii) What is the effect of the use of lists throughout the entire paragraph?

Did you notice the use of the conjunction 'and' linking the lists?

Polysyndetic lists (polysyndeton)

Polysyndetic lists are recognisable by the use of conjunctions (usually 'and' or 'or') between each item. The writer, Ernest Hemingway (1899–1961), was renowned for his use – some would say overuse – of polysyndeton.

The effect of a polysyndetic list is usually to slow the pace of the list, highlighting individually each item in the list, building to a final climax, thus drawing attention to the extent and variety of the items in the list, often culminating in or drawing attention to the final item. There is a sense in which polysyndeton can give the impression of items being piled up, the items being significantly and causally linked.

Here is a simple example: Your mum asks you to go to the shops and buy: carrots and potatoes and leeks and turnip and a treat for yourself. You can see that there is a kind of build-up of vegetables, all linked and all concluding in a final climax – something for yourself!

The following extract is taken from Chapter 3 of *The Sun also Rises* by Ernest Hemingway.

> *It was a warm spring night and I sat at a table on the terrace of the Napolitan after Robert had gone watching it get dark and the electric signs come on, and the red and green stop-and-go traffic-signal, and the crowd going by, and the horse cabs clippety-clopping along at the edge of the solid taxi traffic.*

Hemingway is highly skilled in his use of polysyndetic structure. Look at the number of times he uses 'and' in this long sentence. But what matters is the effect the polysyndetic structure creates: the narrator is sitting watching the darkness descend and then the evening crowds and traffic go past him.

Note how the polysyndetic structure slows the pace thereby conveying in rhythm the slow descent of darkness and the steady movement of the traffic. Also, the structure emphasises each item in the list while creating a build-up, culminating in the final item – 'the horse-cabs, clippety-clopping along the edge of the solid taxi traffic', stressing the noise and activity of the scene.

Quick Test 29

Read the following sentence from Cormac McCarthy's *Cities of the Plain*.

> They stood in the doorway and stomped the rain from their boots and swung their hats and wiped the water from their faces.

Comment on the effect of the polysyndetic structure of the sentence.

Anaphora

Anaphora is a form of lists. It is the repetition of words or phrases at the beginning of sentences and/or clauses), thus creating rhythm and reinforcing the point being made, usually by appealing to feelings and emotions. It is often used to persuade the reader to the writer's ideas and opinions.

Look carefully at this sentence by Robert Louis Stevenson on the weather of Edinburgh:

> *She is liable to be beaten upon by all the winds that blow, to be drenched with rain, to be buried in cold sea fogs out of the east, and powdered with the snow as it comes flying southward from the Highland hills.*

The repetition of the structure – 'to be + past participle': 'to be beaten upon', 'to be drenched with', 'to be buried in', and *'to be* (implied) powdered with' – is a perfect example of anaphora, where the repetition at the beginning of each phrase creates an accumulation of the point being made about the anguish of the Edinburgh weather.

It begins with winds, moves on to the rain, then the sea fogs and finally the snow coming from the north. There is clearly a build-up of appalling conditions, the anaphora intensifying the cumulation of the points being made.

The term *cumulative intensification* is useful to remember when you are commenting on the effect of anaphora or repetition of phrases at the beginning of successive words or phrases or clauses or sentences.

The following example is from George Orwell's essay *Marrakech*. He is talking about the nature of the life of the inhabitants of Morocco:

> *They rise out of the earth, they sweat and starve for a few years, and they sink back into the nameless mounds of the graveyard and nobody notices that they are gone.*

Orwell is a master of this particular kind of sentence structure. The formula is 'They + verb + preposition' as in *They rise out of the earth* and *they sweat* and *starve for a few years...*, a formula which is repeated, in this case, three times. But what is the effect?

In this case, phrases that form the anaphora follow the life cycle of the local people, from birth, through the short years spent working, to an ignominious and anonymous burial. The anaphora captures the formulaic nature of their existence; it also stresses the notion that it is common to them all. It captures the cyclical nature and inevitability of their lives.

> ### Quick Test 30
>
> 1. The following sentence is from an article by Steven Johnson in *The Times*. It concerns the author's views about video games:
>
> > *The gaming universe is literally teeming with objects that deliver very clearly articulated rewards: more life, access to new levels, new equipment, new spells.*
>
>   (i) Identify the writer's use of anaphora.
>   (ii) Comment of the effect of the anaphora.

2. Compose sentences in line with the following techniques by:

   (i) using a list
   (ii) placing phrases at the beginning of the sentence
   (iii) using climax

Tricolon

Tricolon is the name for a list which contains three items. It creates rhythm and therefore reinforces the point being made by emotional appeal. Usually, tricolon also creates climax, highlighting the final item in such a way as to appeal to the reader's emotions.

The number three fascinates us: the three wise monkeys, three blind mice, three wise men, three wishes, three guesses, three little pigs, the three bears.

The following extract is adapted from an online article by Joanna Czechowska about items in the Belfast Titanic Museum:

> *(The museum's) collections reveal what life was like onboard through original artefacts, through stories of the crew and passengers, and the eventual discovery of the wreck.*

Note the three items: 'through original artefacts', 'through stories of the crew and passengers','the eventual discovery of the wreck'. As with any list, the extent of items on display and the variety from stories to bits of the wreck are all revealed. But also note the rhythm created by the tricolon ending in such a sad climax: the discovery of the actual wreck itself.

 Quick Test 31

> *Dinosaurs lived 230 to 66 million years ago through three periods of time known as the Triassic, the Jurassic and the Cretaceous periods.*

1. Comment on the effect of the use of tricolon in this sentence.
2. Compose a sentence in which you use tricolon.

One of the effects of techniques such as lists – anaphora, polysyndetic structure and tricolon – is to create *cumulative intensification*.

Repetition

Repetition is often used to create climactic structure in a sentence, used to intensify the point being made by means of a build-up to an important final point. The repetition can create a steady rhythmical build-up, thereby intensifying meaning – sometimes referred to as a *cumulative or incremental intensification*. Look out for the repetition within a sentence again building up to climax.

You already know about anaphora, where the repetition is of words or phrases or clauses at the beginning of sentences, but there can be repetition within a sentence. For example:

- I asked my friend time and time again to go with me to the cinema.

The repetition of 'time and time' is straightforward but effective in conveying the idea that the request was repeated and probably not fulfilled. Similarly:

- Daddy bear blew and blew on his porridge to try and cool it.

The repetition 'blew and blew' adds more than the simple fact that he blew on his porridge – the repetition suggests that it took some effort and time to attempt to cool his porridge.

> ## Quick Test 32
>
> Read the following sentences and indicate the repetition and comment on the effect:
>
> (i)   I keep telling you and telling you hold the chisel like this.
> (ii) Throughout history there has never ever been such a large dinosaur.
> (iii) That tree will just grow and grow until it is dangerous.

Parenthesis

Parenthesis is another useful common sentence technique (see more details about parenthesis on page 71). It is a method of providing additional information about the point the writer is making. You can recognise parenthesis by the use of paired brackets, paired dashes or paired commas. The additional information is not actually part of the grammar of a sentence – for example:

I went to the shop – the one on the corner – and bought milk.

The parenthesis '– the one in the corner – ' provides additional information but can be removed leaving the sentence grammatically intact: 'I went to the shop and bought milk'. Note that the plural of parenthesis is parentheses.

Parenthesis provides additional information and sometime humour:

Jonathan finally said to the teacher, after thinking for five minutes, that he did not know the answer.

Quick Test 33

1. Read the following sentences and indicate the parenthesis in each and comment on the effect:

   (i)   I play football – only on Wednesdays – in Rovers' ground.
   (ii) I can manage, with a little difficulty, to finish my maths homework.
   (iii) It's worth remembering that Ben Nevis – the highest mountain in the UK – is a very dangerous mountain to climb in winter.

2. Carry out the following tasks:

   (i)   what is a declarative sentence and give an example;
   (ii) what is an imperative sentence and give an example;
   (iii) write a sentence containing a list which illuminates the joys of shopping;
   (iv) explain what is meant by a complex sentence and give an example;
   (v)   write a sentence using parenthesis;
   (vi) write a sentence which is climactic in structure and explain it is effective?

Change in tense

You must be aware of tense when you are analysing sentence structure because skilful writers are able to manipulate tense to achieve the effect of immediacy.

Read the following two paragraphs from an autobiographical piece by William McIlvanney. He remembers how his upbringing was significant in his development as a writer.

> *My mother was a ferocious carer who had an almost mystical capacity to conjure solid worries out of air that to the rest of us looked untroubled and clear. Maybe somebody else was supposed to be with me and had gone out briefly.*
>
> *I don't know. I am simply aware of myself there. The moment sits separate and vivid in my memory, without explanation like a rootless flower. Whoever I was being, traveller or knight, I must have been tired. For I fell asleep.*

Note how the first paragraph is in the past tense, but then McIlvanney switches to the present tense in the second paragraph, thus creating an immediacy as he reflects on the experience which, though it happened some years previously, nevertheless is very much present in his mind.

In the following extract from an article about what could happen if there were to be an impact on Earth from an asteroid, the director, Jay Tate of 'Spaceguard', an organisation set up to look for rogue asteroids, explains what could happen:

> *In the longer term the problem of being hit by an asteroid will be the amount of material that is injected into the Earth's atmosphere. Within two or three days the surface of the Earth will be cold and dark. And it is the dark which will be the problem, because the plants will begin to die out. At best guess, we will probably lose about 25 per cent of the human population in the first six months or so. The rest of us are basically back in the Middle Ages. We have got no power, no communications, no infrastructure. We are back to hunter-gathering.*

Jay Tate begins by using the future tense because he is explaining what might happen as a result of any future impact from a meteor. But then at the sentence beginning 'The rest of us…' he switches to the present tense to dramatise what would happen to those humans who would survive and to create immediacy of the horrors that would be faced.

Quick Test 34

The following extract is from the opening sentence of Michaela Foster March's book *Starchild*:

It's Christmas, 1993. I'm unexpectedly offered a paid three-week vacation back home to Scotland over the holidays. Considering I'm living in Ottawa, Canada, and haven't been home in three years, I don't hesitate.

(i)   Comment on what is surprising about the writer's use of tense.

(ii)   Comment on the effect of her use of tense.

Imperative sentences

An imperative sentence is in the form of a command. Think of the commands given to dogs: Sit! Heel! Or to a badly behaved person – 'Get in here!'. The imperative sentence does not have a subject because the subject is very much implied. For example, 'Tidy your room!'. And the sentence we used on page 47: 'Do not steal porridge!'.

Imperatives can, at times, be used quite subtly as a means of persuading readers. Look at this extract from an article in *The Herald* by Mark Smith:

> *Ask me how I'm feeling. Ask me how I'm feeling after Christmas and New Year and everything it entails. Ask me whether I'm happy or sad or hopeful or depressed and the answer will always be the same. I feel nostalgic. I'm thinking about the past and the used-to-be and I'm wondering: how on earth can I get back there?*

Note that three times he uses the imperative 'Ask me' – persuading the reader to take an interest in *how* he is feeling, all leading to the subject of 'nostalgia' (an affectionate or warm yearning for the past).

It is worth noting his use of anaphora (see pages 61-62) – the three repetitions of 'Ask me', all designed to engage the reader's interest and curiosity, encouraging him/her to read on.

Note also his use of a question at the end of this introductory paragraph. The question is rhetorical… See below!

Questions

There are two main types of questions: rhetorical questions and those that require an answer.

A rhetorical question is a question asked in order to make a point and does not expect an answer. For example, the class is noisy for a second time and the teacher says: 'Do I have to tell you again?'. The teacher most definitely is not expecting and answer but is making a point.

Often, we use rhetorical questions to be persuasive Often questions address the reader directly to allow the reader to think, to consider the point being made. Here is an example from an article by Catherine Bennett about giving 16-year-olds the vote:

> *There are hugely important questions to address before 16-year-olds can be invited into the complicated UK electoral process. Are they sufficiently mature? Can they tell one party from another? Are they too preoccupied by a combination of exams and hectic social lives to be bothered?*

Catherine Bennett asks three questions which are obviously rhetorical. She does not expect the reader to answer them, but she uses them to engage the reader's interest and make him/her think.

Often rhetorical questions are asked at the beginning of articles in order to engage a reader and persuade him/her to read on.

 Quick Test 35

You are writing an article about the wearing of school uniform for your school magazine. Write the introduction in no more than two paragraphs and include two or three rhetorical questions.

A balanced sentence is where two parts of a sentence are equal but separated by a semi-colon or a conjunction to create symmetry (evenness/balance). The two parts are usually equal in length, in importance and in structure. Take J F Kennedy's famous remark:

> *When the going gets tough, the tough get going.*

The balance is almost perfect – the two clauses separated by the comma are balanced, but so are the words 'tough' and 'going'.

Some writers can use balanced sentences to create humorous effect. Take this quotation by Oscar Wilde:

> *Some cause happiness wherever they go; others, whenever they go.*

The balance is obvious, the semi-colon the perfect pivot. The idea that some people only cause happiness once they leave company is pointed up by the balance. But this sentence also uses contrast - 'some' and 'others'; as well as 'wherever' and 'whenever'.

And

> *The truth is rarely pure and never simple.*

Again, note the use of contrast between 'rarely' and 'never'; and 'pure' and simple'.

When looking for contrast, look for contrasting words, of course, but look for conjunctions that can signal contrast – 'but', 'although', 'whereas', 'yet'. For example:

> *Although Jonathan is tall, his sister is quite short.*

When analysing sentences, look for balance and contrast. It is possible that you may be asked about how contrast is established, in which case look for balance and/or words signalling contrast.

Read carefully the following extract from an article by Matthew Syed. He is talking about the kind of pressure that top footballers face when about to take a penalty. They claim that:

> *"Pressure is not a problem; it is a privilege". Talk to David Beckham, Sebastian Coe or Sir Chris Hoy and they will be perfectly open about their nerves and fear. But they also talk with great pride about facing up to them. They didn't see these human responses as signs of weakness but as opportunities to grow.*

Note the balance in 'Pressure is not a problem; it is a privilege': but also note the contrast of 'pressure' (something unpleasant) and 'privilege' (something positive), making the saying almost a paradox (what appears to be a contradiction), the point of which is to make the reader think about the truth of what is being said. (Note also the alliteration of the 'p', which further draws attention to the phrase.)

The writer uses 'But' at the beginning of 'But they also talk…', which introduces the contrast between 'nerves and fear' and 'facing up to them', and also the 'but' in the next sentence highlights the contrast between 'weakness' and 'opportunities to grow'.

The use of the imperative – 'Talk to' – has the effect of addressing and involving the reader. Note also the repetition (anaphora) of 'they talk', which has the effect of reinforcing the affirmative nature of the sportsmen's attitudes.

When analysing sentence structure, keep in mind balance and contrast and sentences which compare – they are all used more frequently than we realise.

Look for **structures of comparisons**: 'Although X is the case, Y is also the case', 'Not only is X the case, but Y is also the case'.

Structures signalling balance: 'On the one hand X is the case, and on the other …'. Often sentences using balance and comparisons use similar structures.

Structures of contrast: 'Whereas X is the case, nevertheless Y is different'. 'X is the case, yet Y is different', and of course the use of 'but' which signals a change or contrast.

Punctuation – Commas

There aren't really any *rules* concerning punctuation, but punctuation can signal meaning, making what is being said much clearer to the reader.

Look at these two sentences

(i) Let's eat Aunt Patsy.

(ii) Let's eat, Aunt Patsy.

Do you spot the difference the comma makes? It stops you being caught up in cannibalism.

The importance of the correct use of punctuation cannot be stressed enough.

Commas

The comma has several important uses.

Commas when addressing someone

For example, 'Hello, Mr MacKenzie, I'm here to collect the shopping.'

Or, 'I'm sorry, Aunt Patsy, I didn't mean to scare you.'

Because you are addressing these people, their names need commas before and after.

Quick Test 36

What is the difference in meaning between:
- I think he is someone I don't know.
- I think he is someone, I don't know.

Commas used to separate two main clauses

A compound sentence consists of two (or more) main clauses joined by a conjunction:

- Darren read the book, but his friend preferred watching football.
- Mum likes TV, but my sister prefers the cinema.

Where there are two main clauses linked by a conjunction, you should use a comma before the conjunction, as in the examples above. You need the comma even if the grammatical subject is repeated:

- I went to the supermarket, and I was appalled at how busy it was.

Commas used to signal parenthesis (see page 64 above)

Paired commas are used (as well as paired brackets or paired dashes) to signal parenthesis. Parenthesis is when information is added to the sentence without being part of the grammar – the sentence still exists intact without the parenthetical phrase. For example:

- I went to the shop, the one in the next street, only to find it closed.

The additional information 'the one on the corner' can be removed without affecting the sentence grammatically. The commas can be replaced with dashes or brackets:

- I went to the shop (the one on the corner) only to find it closed.
- I went to the shop – the one on the corner – only to find it closed.

Another example:

- Students, it has to be said, haven't had it easy this year.

The use of parenthesis is much more common than you think.

Commas used to indicate a break in normal syntactical order

Syntax is the set of rules that creates a recognisable sentence.

We often break normal sentence order in order to create emphasis by placing a word or phrase or even a subordinate clause at the beginning of a sentence. We saw such syntactical arrangement on pages 51-52.

Look at the sentence:

- Slowly, the young man crossed the river on a paddle board.

Normal syntax would place the adverb next to the verb:

- The young man slowly crossed the river on a paddle board

Because we have broken normal word order we have to use a comma after 'Slowly'.

We could change the sentence round again:

- On a paddle board, slowly, the young man crossed the river.

Note the commas indicating the break in normal word order.

Commas used to separate items in lists

Commas are used to separate items in a list. For example:

- There were almond orchards, fields of pomegranates, pistachios, grapes and apricots.

There is a comma separating each item, though in this example there is no comma before the conjunction.

YET sometimes it is important to have a comma before the conjunction. Such comma is referred to as the Oxford (or serial) comma. It is used when the writer wants to indicate that the penultimate (second-last) and ultimate items really are separate.

Its use can avoid confusion. Look at the following:

- I love my parents, Annie Lennox and Robbie Williams.

Without the comma, that could read that Annie Lennox and Robbie Williams are my parents! The Oxford (or serial) comma clears matters:

- I love my parents, Annie Lennox, and Robbie Williams.

The use of the Oxford comma also makes clear when the last two items are separate:

- In your answer, you should consider the following poetic techniques: sound, imagery, rhythm and rhyme.

The student may be left wondering if rhythm and rhyme should be dealt with together or separately. The Oxford comma solves the problem:

- In your answer, you should consider the following poetic techniques: sound, imagery, rhythm, and rhyme.

Commas used to signal apposition

Apposition is where two or more words or phrases are in parallel and share the same referent; that is, refer to the same thing. For example:

- Brad Pitt, the famous movie star, said today…

The phrase 'the famous movie star' and the term 'Brad Pitt' are identical and 'the famous movie star' is in apposition to 'Brad Pitt'.

Let's take another example:

- My best friend, George, goes to the cinema every Friday.

In effect, there are two subjects of the verb 'goes' ('My best friend' and 'George'), though they are one and the same person. Because the two subjects are in parallel, the second noun must be separated by commas.

The word or phrase that is in apposition must be isolated by paired commas.

REMEMBER

Punctuation is there to signal/clarify meaning!

BUT – watch out for the comma splice

Comma splice

One of the most common errors in writing is the use of the comma splice where a writer uses a comma to 'splice' two main clauses, not realising that the comma is not strong enough to join main clauses. In your essay writing, check to make sure you do not use a comma splice.

Look at this example:

- I have a dog, its name is Mandy.

The comma after 'dog' **cannot** join these two main clauses. The clauses are: 'I have a dog' and 'its name is Mandy'.

Clearly, these two units of sense are connected and can be joined, but not by a comma. How can we join them?

By keeping them as two separate sentences:

- I have a dog. Its name is Mandy.

By using *and*:

- I have a dog and its name is Mandy.

But that sounds a bit childish.

By using the relative pronoun (for example: which, who, whose, that):

- I have a dog whose name is Mandy.

By using the semi-colon:

- I have a dog; its name is Mandy.

The semi-colon is by far the best way of indicating the connection between the ideas; moreover, it is also a very stylish punctuation mark.

The semi-colon is strong enough to join to related main clauses – and its use will give your writing flair and style.

Semi-colon

The semi-colon is a punctuation mark that is as underrated as it is underused. It is an incredibly useful and stylish piece of punctuation that can do much to clarify meaning and enhance your writing.

The semi-colon has three main uses.

Joining two or more related main clauses

This particular use of the semi-colon is illustrated above. It can be used to indicate an interconnection between main clauses which in themselves could stand as grammatically independent sentences. See above.

The semi-colon is not only a useful punctuation mark; it adds style to your writing.

Separating items in a complex list

In a list where commas are already used, the semi-colon can clarify separate larger items.

The following example is from the introduction to a book called *IMPACT! The Threat of Comets and Asteroids* by Gerrit L Verschuur:

> For more than two centuries, the possibility that the Earth might be struck by comets has been debated, and three questions have been raised from the start: will a comet again hit the Earth; might comet impact lead to the extinction of mankind; is it possible that the flood legends from so many world cultures could be explained by past comet impact in the oceans which triggered enormous tsunamis?

Each of these three questions is quite long and a comma would be insufficient and even confusing whereas the semi-colon makes clear that there are three separate questions.

Creating balance

A fairly rare, but highly polished use of the semi-colon is to create balance between two separate but related units of sense. For example:

> To err is human; to forgive divine.

The semi-colon is a much underused and underrated punctuation mark, which can add style and great clarity to your writing.

Colon

The mighty colon has four uses:

Introducing a list

Here is an example from an article by Gerry Hassan in the Scottish Review:

> *Peter Jackson's film about the Beatles reveals aspects of their relationships: their chemistry, bonds, history, creative processes and how they connected.*

The colon signals the list that indicates the aspects of their relationships.

Signalling an explanation or an example after a statement

In the above example the colon introduces a list, but it also introduces the explanation of what is meant by 'their relationships'. The best way of thinking about this use of the colon is to think in terms of 'statement: explanation' or 'statement: example'.

Introducing a quotation

For example:

> *On the balcony of her father's house, Juliet wondered: 'Wherefore art thou, Romeo?'*

Separating numbers – as in time

> *Your appointment is at 16:15.*

The colon is also a very useful punctuation mark: after a statement, it can signal an explanation or an example. Using the colon reveals a sophisticated and knowledgeable writer.

Punctuation of direct speech

A rule of direct speech is that each new speaker – or the words leading up to a new speaker – must form a new line or a new paragraph.

For example:

> "How are you today?" asked Ryan.
>
> "Fine," replied Steven. "How are you?"
>
> "I am looking forward to going back to school," laughed Ryan.
>
> Steven scowled, "I'm not!"
>
> "Oh come on, Stephen, at least we'll see our friends for the first time in months."

Note the position of the punctuation marks. Note also that the first word of a new sentences requires a capital letter.

Make sure there is a full stop at the end of sentences, unless you use question or exclamation marks.

In the punctuation of direct speech, the full stop, question mark or exclamation mark is placed inside the inverted commas.

Quick Test 37

Using direct speech set a conversation you have with your friend about your new phone.

In the school canteen, you are a witness to some boisterous horseplay involving food being thrown about. The head teacher calls you to describe the event – think of the language you would use when speaking to him/her. You then meet your best friend on the way home. You retell the story to him/her of the events in the canteen. Do you use exactly the same language that you used with the head teacher? Or do you modify your language according to whoever you are speaking to?

Register is the way we adjust our sentence structure, vocabulary, greetings, and how we address people according to a given social setting or context. It is the language (sentences, phrases, words) we consider appropriate for a given audience or reader. The kind of language – sentence structure, phrases, words – that is appropriate for your best friend's ears just might not be so appropriate for the head teacher's.

It's the same with texts and emails where the mode – the nature of texts and emails (speed, space constraints, informality) not only creates its own register but also creates the opportunity for a different kind of spelling where vowels can replace entire words ('u' for 'you'), numbers can replace words ('2' for 'to') and replace syllables (as in 'str8' for 'straight', 'm8' for 'mate', and 'b4' for 'before'). Sometimes vowels are completely omitted ('txt' for 'text' and 'rtn' for 'return') and sometimes letters are used to stand for entire words ('brb' for 'be right back' and 'lol' for 'laughing out loud' or 'lots of love').

The following diagram might help:

Formal writing	Informal writing
(less like spoken English)	(more like spoken English)
formal constructions	informal constructions
complex-compound sentences	simple sentences
use of subordination/inversion	minor sentences
no contractions/abbreviations	slang/colloquialisms
long sentences	short sentences
use of colons and semi-colons	simple punctuation

(i)   List social media platforms where the use of informal register is appropriate and acceptable.

(ii) Give an example of a social media message using informal register.

(iii) Choose a subject that interests you and write a paragraph in formal register.

Remember that register is determined by the social or language context. In any given day, you may use several different registers.

Tone

Sometimes you asked about the tone of a piece of writing. Tone conveys a writer's attitude to whatever they are writing about. Ask yourself: is the writer using a tone of disapproval or annoyance or approval or humour or even sarcasm? Is the tone serious or sad? To work out tone you have to analyse the language being used.

Read the following extract from an article in the *Guardian*. The writer is arguing that we overprotect our children and should 'set them free':

> *Stop popping the balloons. Forget the dew on the grass. Bring back the conkers and the yo-yos. And ditch those hi-vis jackets that make every child look like Bob the Builder. It's time, says the chief inspector of schools, to blast the bugles, sound the trumpets and chuck out the cotton wool. It's time, in fact, to set the children of this nation free.*

The writer is clearly using humour. Her use of imperatives at the beginning – 'Stop', 'Forget', Bring back' - is intended to arrest the reader's attention and engage him/her, and the weirdness of 'Forget the dew on the grass' and 'Bring back the conkers' immediately makes us smile. Word choice such as 'yo-yos', 'ditch', 'hi-vis jackets', 'Bob the Builder' add to the humorous tone. The list – 'to blast the bugles, sound the trumpets and chuck out the cotton wool' – are humorous because of their exaggeration (the first two items in the list) and the anticlimax (the opposite of climax) of 'chuck out the cotton wool'.

The following is an extract from an article in the then Sunday Herald about the importance of city squares:

> *At their best, public squares are the beating heart of the city: a magnet for overseas visitors, a place where local people gather informally from day to day, or at those critical, historic times which define a city, or even a country.*

The tone of this paragraph is one of approval – note phrases such as 'At their best', where the superlative 'best' suggests city squares can be of the highest quality, the most pleasing aspect of a city; they can be the 'beating heart of the city', where 'beating heart' suggests vibrant life, the place which pumps life throughout the city. He approves of the city square because it is a 'place where local people gather informally from day to day', thus giving people an opportunity to meet casually and intimately. A square also 'defines a city' or 'country' during significant moments in a country's development by having people to gather in such a central place.

Quick Test 39

1. In the following extract by the same writer, show, by reference to language, how he expresses his tone of dismay about the failure of George Square.

Why then, have we failed so dismally to design the bold and beautiful civic spaces that characterise the world's greatest cities? As other cities continue to nurture, renew and regenerate their great civic spaces, or even create splendid new ones, Scotland again stumbles, staggers and slumps into another embarrassing demonstration of how not to do it. George Square, currently dominated by traffic, is a crossing point rather than a gathering place. In the evenings, it doesn't function as other city squares do.

Write a paragraph in which you express dismay about some aspect of where you live.

2. The writer Rebecca McQuillan writes in *The Herald* about the Americanisation of English. Here is an extract from the article:

"Hey buddy. Doin' good?" "Sure, I'm fine. Covid sucks but it's Christmas, right?"

When you overhear an exchange like that in your local shop between two people with broad Scottish accents, it's time to lodge an official complaint.

The British habit of cloning American dialogue seems to have reached new heights. Months bingeing on Netflix, Disney Plus and Hollywood films appear to have had the effect of a full immersion language course. Some of us seem to be living and breathing American English.

   (i) Analyse the extent to which the opening paragraph is in the register of formal or informal English.

   (ii) Read the second paragraph.

With reference to sentence structure, analyse how the writer reveals her annoyance at the Americanisation of English.

   (iii) Read the third paragraph.

Comment on the tone the writer is using and say, with reference to language, how she makes that tone clear.

Answers

Answers to the Quick tests and a glossary of useful terms are available online. Visit
https://collins.co.uk/pages/scottish-curriculum-free-resources-leckie-snap-revision